CAROLINE BIRD

Multi-award-winning poet and playwright Caroline Bird is from Leeds and lives in Rochester. She has had six collections of poetry published by Carcanet: *Looking Through Letterboxes* (2002); *Trouble Came to the Turnip* (2006); *Watering Can* (2009); *The Hat-Stand Union* (2013); *In These Days of Prohibition* (2017), which was shortlisted for the T.S. Eliot Prize and the Ted Hughes Award, and *The Air Year* (2020), which won the Forward Prize for Best Collection 2020 and was shortlisted for the Costa Prize and the Polari Prize. Her poems have been published in anthologies and journals, and broadcast on BBC Radio 4 and Radio 3. She was one of five official poets at the London 2012 Olympics.

Caroline began writing plays as a teenager and was the youngest ever member of the Royal Court Young Writers' Programme. She has been shortlisted for the Susan Smith Blackburn Prize, and as Most Promising New Playwright at the Off-West-End Awards. Her plays include *The Trial of Dennis the Menace* (Southbank Centre); *The Trojan Women* (Gate Theatre); *Chamber Piece* (Lyric Theatre Hammersmith) and *The Wonderful Wizard of Oz* (Northern Stage). *Red Ellen*, was shortlisted for the 2021 George Devine Award, recognising new writing and powerful voices.

Other Titles in this Series

Mike Bartlett
THE 47TH
ALBION
BULL
GAME
AN INTERVENTION
KING CHARLES III
MRS DELGADO
SCANDALTOWN
SNOWFLAKE
VASSA *after* Gorky
WILD

Chris Bush
THE ASSASSINATION OF KATIE HOPKINS
THE CHANGING ROOM
FAUSTUS: THAT DAMNED WOMAN
HUNGRY
JANE EYRE *after* Brontë
THE LAST NOËL
STEEL

Jez Butterworth
THE FERRYMAN
JERUSALEM
JEZ BUTTERWORTH PLAYS: ONE
JEZ BUTTERWORTH PLAYS: TWO
MOJO
THE NIGHT HERON
PARLOUR SONG
THE RIVER
THE WINTERLING

Caryl Churchill
BLUE HEART
CHURCHILL PLAYS: THREE
CHURCHILL PLAYS: FOUR
CHURCHILL PLAYS: FIVE
CHURCHILL: SHORTS
CLOUD NINE
DING DONG THE WICKED
A DREAM PLAY *after* Strindberg
DRUNK ENOUGH TO SAY I LOVE YOU?
ESCAPED ALONE
FAR AWAY
GLASS. KILL. BLUEBEARD'S FRIENDS.
    IMP.
HERE WE GO
HOTEL
ICECREAM
LIGHT SHINING IN BUCKINGHAMSHIRE
LOVE AND INFORMATION
MAD FOREST
A NUMBER
PIGS AND DOGS
SEVEN JEWISH CHILDREN
THE SKRIKER
THIS IS A CHAIR
THYESTES *after* Seneca
TRAPS
WHAT IF IF ONLY

debbie tucker green
BORN BAD
DEBBIE TUCKER GREEN PLAYS: ONE
DIRTY BUTTERFLY
EAR FOR EYE
HANG
NUT
A PROFOUNDLY AFFECTIONATE,
    PASSIONATE DEVOTION TO
    SOMEONE (– NOUN)
RANDOM
STONING MARY
TRADE & GENERATIONS
TRUTH AND RECONCILIATION

Chris Hannan
CRIME AND PUNISHMENT
    after Dostoyevsky
ELIZABETH GORDON QUINN
THE GOD OF SOHO
SHINING SOULS
WHAT SHADOWS

Branden Jacobs-Jenkins
APPROPRIATE
GLORIA
AN OCTOROON

Cordelia Lynn
HEDDA TESMAN *after* Ibsen
LELA & CO.
LOVE AND OTHER ACTS OF VIOLENCE
ONE FOR SORROW
THREE SISTERS *after* Chekhov

Lucy Kirkwood
BEAUTY AND THE BEAST
    with Katie Mitchell
BLOODY WIMMIN
THE CHILDREN
CHIMERICA
HEDDA *after* Ibsen
IT FELT EMPTY WHEN THE HEART
    WENT AT FIRST BUT IT IS
    ALRIGHT NOW
LUCY KIRKWOOD PLAYS: ONE
MOSQUITOES
NSFW
TINDERBOX
THE WELKIN

Winsome Pinnock
LEAVE TAKING
ROCKETS AND BLUE LIGHTS
TAKEN
TITUBA

Stef Smith
ENOUGH
GIRL IN THE MACHINE
HUMAN ANIMALS
NORA : A DOLL'S HOUSE
REMOTE
SWALLOW

Sophie Swithinbank
BACON

Jack Thorne
2ND MAY 1997
AFTER LIFE
BUNNY
BURYING YOUR BROTHER IN
    THE PAVEMENT
A CHRISTMAS CAROL *after* Dickens
THE END OF HISTORY…
HOPE
JACK THORNE PLAYS: ONE
JUNKYARD
LET THE RIGHT ONE IN
    after John Ajvide Lindqvist
MYDIDAE
THE SOLID LIFE OF SUGAR WATER
STACY & FANNY AND FAGGOT
WHEN YOU CURE ME
WOYZECK *after* Büchner

Phoebe Waller-Bridge
FLEABAG

Joy Wilkinson
ACTING LEADER
FAIR & FELT EFFECTS
THE SWEET SCIENCE OF BRUISING

Caroline Bird

RED ELLEN

NICK HERN BOOKS
London
www.nickhernbooks.co.uk

A Nick Hern Book

Red Ellen first published in Great Britain in 2022 as a paperback original by Nick Hern Books Limited, The Glasshouse, 49a Goldhawk Road, London W12 8QP

Red Ellen copyright © 2022 Caroline Bird

Caroline Bird has asserted her right to be identified as the author of this work

Cover design by Velcrobelly (www.velcrobelly.co.uk)

Designed and typeset by Nick Hern Books, London
Printed in Great Britain by Mimeo Ltd, Huntingdon, Cambridgeshire PE29 6XX

A CIP catalogue record for this book is available from the British Library

ISBN 978 1 83904 066 5

Woodland CARBON
www.woodlandcarbon.co.uk
NICK HERN BOOKS
Printed on Carbon Captured paper

Red Ellen was first co-produced by Northern Stage, Nottingham Playhouse and Royal Lyceum Edinburgh, and performed at Northern Stage, Newcastle upon Tyne, from 25 March 2022, before touring to the other venues and to York Theatre Royal. The cast was as follows:

ELLEN	Bettrys Jones
ANNIE	Helen Katamba
DAVID	Jim Kitson
ISABEL	Laura Evelyn
OTTO	Sandy Batchelor
HERBERT	Kevin Lennon
MR ANSLEY	Mercedes Assad

All other parts played by members of the company

Director	Wils Wilson
Set and Costume Designer	Camilla Clarke
Music and Sound Designer	Jasmin Kent Rodgman
Lighting Designer	Kai Fischer
Movement Director	Patricia Suarez
Intimacy Director	Vanessa Coffey
Fight Director	Kaitlin Howard
Dramaturg	Kate Leys
Wardrobe Supervisor	Naomi Daley
Assistant Director (*RTYDS*)	Bex Bowsher
Production Manager	Marty Moore
Stage Manager	Alec Reece
Deputy Stage Manager	Nichola Mecrow
Assistant Stage Manager	Grace Branch
Dresser	Laura Jane Aitman

Characters

ELLEN WILKINSON, *born 1891. Between the ages of forty-one and fifty-five in this play*

ANNIE WILKINSON, *Ellen's older sister. Born 1881. Between the ages of fifty-one and sixty-five in this play*

HERBERT MORRISON, *Labour politician, Leader of London County Council, the party's leading anti-Communist. Born 1888. Between the ages of forty-four and fifty-eight in this play*

OTTO KATZ, *Comintern Agent, Czechoslovakian, Soviet propagandist. Born 1895. Between the ages of thirty-seven and fifty-one in this play*

ISABEL BROWN, *British Communist activist, secretary of The Relief Committee for the Victims of German Fascism. Born 1894. Between the ages of thirty-nine and forty-eight in this play*

DAVID, *local man from Jarrow. Sheet metal worker, now unemployed. Fifty-one in his scene*

MARY, *a young woman from the tenements in the East End of London, with four children. Thirties*

LILY, *Mary's mother, also a lifelong East Ender, with six children. Early sixties*

WINSTON CHURCHILL, *born 1874. Sixty-six years old in his scene*

MR ANSLEY, *a representative for the Jarrow Labour Exchange. Any age. Possibly young*

ALBERT EINSTEIN, *born 1894. Forty years old in his scene*

ERNEST HEMINGWAY, *American novelist. Born 1899. Thirty-seven years old in his scene*

JOHN DOS PASSOS, *American novelist. Born 1896. Forty years old in his scene*

Note on Text

A forward slash (/) indicates an interruption.

Notes on Play

The play spans the last fourteen years of Ellen's life (1933–47).

Can be played by seven actors or more, doubling parts.

As Ellen's height (4ft 9in) was such a distinct and commented-upon feature it is important that the actor playing her is similar in height.

Other minor characters can be played by the cast.

Notes on Ellen

It was remarked upon that Ellen was always falling over in the Houses of Parliament due to running in the corridors… So, where possible, she should literally run from scene to scene, falling over occasionally, picking herself up, running again… This should feel real and slightly worrying, not farcical.

Where possible, in every scene she should be wearing a different outfit; although she will probably have to change on the run. Her outfits start out bright and bold, but then the colours become darker (after the Spanish Civil War) as she progresses upwards in her parliamentary career.

Ellen was a very heavy smoker. I have occasionally written her smoking into the stage directions but not always. Throughout the play she should be smoking more often than not. She also drinks a huge amount of coffee.

The combination of her innate spirit and the adrenaline in her asthma medication means Ellen can't keep still; even when standing on the spot there is a sense of motion within her, always looking for something to do, fiddle with, access, observe. Even thinking is a physical act for her, thoughts visibly rippling across her face.

Finally, Ellen was labelled 'fiery' and 'passionate' by other people, mainly men, but there was obviously something a lot more complex and mercurial happening. To inspire action in others, a woman must often duck and weave, switch tones, keep the air around themselves nimble and unpredictable. She was fiery, yes, but a thousand other adjectives too.

'Jarrow March' song

Music by	Jasmin Kent Rodgman
Lyrics	Caroline Bird
Choir	The Felling Male Voice Choir
Vocalist	Kate Doherty

This text went to press before the end of rehearsals and so may differ slightly from the play as performed.

ACT ONE

Scene One

Summer 1933, Labour Party Conference.

ELLEN. Throughout this conference, I have been haunted by our incomprehensible inaction. Fascism is knocking at the door of the world and where are we? All tucked up, swaddled in the assumption that life as we have always known it in these islands is going on. The Reichstag went up in flames this year, Germany is a police state with a barbarian anti-Jewish policy and yet we, the Labour Party, are barely even talking about it. And why is that? Because the anti-fascist movement in Britain is largely funded by the Communist Party and any association with the Far Left would play badly for us in the voting booths. Indeed, I can see Herbert Morrison's ears glowing from here at the mere thought of a 'united front'. (I sincerely hope, when he reaches the Pearly Gates, Saint Peter can reassure him there are no Soviets inside.) People are dying. And what is the government doing? Nothing. And most of the House of Lords openly *admire* Hitler. Are we planning, as the opposition, to be equally ineffective? Where is our team spirit? Where is our energy and drive? Squabbling on the Left strengthens the Right. The tide of fascism is rising, and we need all hands on deck.

HERBERT *stands up slowly.*

HERBERT. Miss Wilkinson says we should act with more energy and drive. She is amply possessed of both. Although sometimes it goes into the wrong channels and she is a bit of nuisance to us.

ELLEN. Sorry, Mum.

HERBERT. Perhaps Miss Wilkinson – instead of running around with people whom she knows are nothing but trouble – might be better occupied concentrating her undoubted 'energy and drive' on the electoral chances of her *own* party.

ELLEN*'s speaking time is over so she cannot retaliate.*

Scene Two

The Café Royal – a favourite London hangout for Communist intellectuals.

ELLEN *and* ISABEL *at their customary table, on their third bottle of wine…*

ELLEN. Party politics is this massive game of tiddlywinks now, tiny little tiny tiny moves, everyone wants to be the master tiddlywinker, no bravery, no bold decisions, just /

ISABEL. Tiddling with their winkers.

ELLEN. Wahey!

ISABEL. Communists are the only ones who care.

ELLEN. Oi, I care.

ISABEL. Your party doesn't.

ELLEN. They're scared.

ISABEL. Of us? We're the heroes of the Left: the revolutionaries, the internationalists, the marchers, bucket-rattlers, radical publishers /

ELLEN. Rabble-rousers.

ISABEL. If a rabble wants rousing, we'll do it. The Communist Party is fighting fascism twenty-five hours a day.

ELLEN. You spat right in my eye.

ISABEL. Sorry.

ELLEN. Quite liked it. Tangible passion.

ISABEL. Top-up?

ELLEN. You can't waste a booth in the Café Royal.

ISABEL. Virginia Woolf was in here earlier, tight as a nun's chuff. I said, 'Would you like to write a cheque for the anti-fascist cause?' She said, 'I'm sorry I don't have a pen.' I said, 'You poor soul, a writer without a pen, please keep mine, you can use it for your next novel about miserable posh people.' But she was gone.

ELLEN *laughs*.

The British ruling classes would rather see Hitler come to power than the social changes brought about by the classes that oppose him. That is the truth.

ELLEN. But this is what I don't understand, Isabel. Labour *isn't* the ruling classes...

ISABEL. Then they should stop acting like it.

ELLEN. They're being 'cautious'.

ISABEL. A coward's favourite word.

ELLEN. Because the country sees socialism as this failed project. We were an impotent minority government for two years and then we resigned in disgrace. So, now, we must 'win back public trust'.

ISABEL. Urgh, the public.

ELLEN. We can't look too left-wing. We need an easily digestible 'clear narrative'.

ISABEL. Start compromising now, you'll never stop.

ELLEN. They tell me, 'Pick your battles, Ellen.' No. When the world is burning, you put out the flames; you don't run around with your hose choosing between fires. If I was running the Labour Party...

ISABEL. Which you will...

ELLEN. ONE DAY. I'll say, to hell with caution. To hell with a safe little electable watered-down trickle of a stance.

OTTO KATZ *appears at* ELLEN'*s shoulder, carrying three shot glasses*.

OTTO. We have a world to win.

ELLEN. Jesus Christ.

OTTO. Almost. Ladies...

ISABEL. No, bollocks, you've ruined it.

OTTO. What?

ISABEL. 'Ladies.' Vodka shots. Jauntily angled hat. Get out.

OTTO. This is Becherovka, nectar of my homeland, made from a secret Czechoslovakian recipe. Greetings to my fellow alumni of the Lenin School, Isabel Brown. And *special* greetings to the imminent Ellen Wilkinson of whom I have heard so much.

ISABEL. Eminent.

OTTO. Hmm?

ISABEL. Not imminent. Eminent.

OTTO *whips a tiny notebook from his inside jacket pocket, quickly writes the word 'eminent', then slips the notebook back in his pocket.*

ELLEN. I am imminently eminent.

ISABEL. I'm so sorry, Ellen, this isn't a suave Soviet set-up, I promise, I just thought you two should meet like normal people.

ELLEN. Who are you?

OTTO. Who aren't I?

ISABEL. This is Otto Katz. Director of anti-fascist propaganda.

OTTO. I am the master of ceremonies.

ISABEL. He's a prick, but he gets things done. Otto is action personified.

ELLEN. Oh really?

ISABEL. And so's Ellen. Action meet Action.

ELLEN. Sounds messy.

OTTO. How do you do?

ELLEN. I am a Labour politician. And I plan to stand for election again, as a *Labour* MP. So…

ISABEL. We're not recruiting you.

OTTO. Oh God no. This isn't about switching sides, Miss Wilkinson…

ISABEL. Straddle both sides.

OTTO. Like skiing. One socialist ski, one anti-fascist ski.

ELLEN. Missed a decent pun on 'Trot-ski' there.

ISABEL. Yeah but /

OTTO. We don't really like him any more /

ISABEL. Anyway /

OTTO. My point is: whoosh.

ELLEN. Your point is whoosh?

OTTO. We are setting up a new committee.

ELLEN. With a snappy title?

ISABEL. The Relief Committee for the Victims of German Fascism.

OTTO. And we'd like you to run it.

ISABEL. Alongside me.

OTTO. Dazzle the crowds at our fundraisers. Rescue refugees. Publish anti-fascist literature. If you want to fight Hitler, don't 'wait' for your party to grant you permission.

ELLEN. Which they won't…

OTTO. Our movement is just that: *movement*. What do you say?

Beat.

ISABEL. Ellen is understandably cautious.

ELLEN *downs her shot of Becherovka.*

ELLEN. I'm in.

Scene Three

The cottage in Buckinghamshire that ELLEN *and* ANNIE *rent.*
ANNIE *lives there full-time,* ELLEN *visits whenever she can –*
weekends here and there.

ANNIE *is fitting* ELLEN *for a bright-red woollen dress.*

ANNIE. Stay still.

ELLEN. I am still.

ANNIE. You've lost weight.

ELLEN. I haven't.

ANNIE. Oh, sorry this must be one of those subjective tape
measures, my mistake.

Beat.

What was it Mum used to say? Food is fuel.

ELLEN. So's coffee.

ANNIE *gives her a little shove.*

Yes, yes.

ANNIE. Now I know red is risky for a redhead but this is
Ellen-Red. I picked it out special from the wool shop. I said,
'Could I please have the faded blood of fallen comrades
mixed with lipstick mixed with the leather interior of an
Austin 7 mixed with Heinz tomato soup?'

Beat.

Don't crack your face, will you?

ELLEN. What?

ANNIE. You've got a tremor in your leg.

ELLEN. I'm thinking.

ANNIE. Ahhh, a thought tremor. Silly me.

Beat.

So I made friends with this really interesting woman in the
village called Petula, she's half-French, also unmarried,
obscenely lovely handwriting with curly calligraphy bits.

Anyway, we shared a sherry and I was laughing like
I haven't laughed in /

ELLEN. I *am* stressed about work.

ANNIE. Right.

ELLEN. It's too much.

ANNIE. Could you take on… less?

ELLEN. Less what?

ANNIE. Work.

ELLEN. It's all vital.

ANNIE. So what are you going to do?

ELLEN. About what?

ANNIE. Being overworked?

ELLEN. What do you mean?

Beat.

ANNIE. I've changed your sheets. I know you only slept here
once last month but it's nicer to have freshly / cleaned

ELLEN. Maybe I'm not stressed maybe I'm lonely. I don't feel
supported, professionally. I just want someone – one person!
– to be unconditionally on my side. Is that too much to ask?

ANNIE. No…

ELLEN. In bed, me and Frank, we had this thing /

ANNIE. Don't.

ELLEN. He'd hold my face in both hands, scan my eyes, and
say, 'It's me and you.'

ANNIE. It's Me and You and My Wife.

ELLEN. Oh – She wasn't even…

ANNIE. Me, You, My Wife and My Secretary.

ELLEN. My secretary, she was MY secretar–…

ELLEN *gasps for breath.*

ANNIE. We talked about this. Emotion provokes your asthma.

ELLEN. Then I'm allergic to my own life.

ANNIE. Just. Look. After. Yourself.

ELLEN. I've bigger things to worry about.

ANNIE *stabs her with a pin*.

OWWW. Police!

ANNIE. Ellen, you do know there's nothing shameful about being ill?

ELLEN. Annie's intense face.

ANNIE. It's the world that's wrong, not you.

ELLEN (*looking down at the dress*). I'm not sure about this colour.

ANNIE. Oh.

ELLEN. Aren't I blending into my own hair?

ANNIE. Maybe a bit.

ELLEN. I look like I'm on fire. It's not me. It's too… one thing. Sorry.

ANNIE. It's fine. Are you staying?

ELLEN. Till four, then back / to London

ANNIE. That's not a day off.

ELLEN. You know that feeling when you wake up and your jaw aches? Like you've been holding onto a rope between your teeth all night? And your first thought is, how am I ever going to stop this?

ANNIE. Stop what?

ELLEN. Fascism. Unemployment. Hunger. Everything. Come on, that feeling, when your eyes are like smashed windows and you can feel the threat to humanity like this this this this terrible wind blowing through yourself. Don't you ever feel like that?

Beat.

ANNIE. No, not really.

Scene Four

ELLEN*'s flat on Guilford Street, Bloomsbury. A charming little one-roomed flat with orange cups and saucers, blue mugs and hand-painted blue chairs. A warm and cosy oasis.*

OTTO *and* ELLEN *rush in, falling through the door, out of breath and exhilarated.*

ELLEN. Oh my... WHOA.

OTTO. I'm dizzy.

ELLEN. Good Lord.

OTTO. It was like riding a hurricane.

ELLEN. I think it was the second spin that did it.

OTTO. You were a devil on that roundabout. An absolute devil.

ELLEN. And you were screaming like a chimpanzee on fire.

OTTO. AHHHHHHHHHHHHHHHH.

ELLEN. AHHHHHHHHHHHHHHHH.

OTTO *runs to the window and twitches back the curtains.*

OTTO. Wait, wait.

ELLEN. What?

OTTO. There's a parked car.

ELLEN. Where?

OTTO. There.

ELLEN. It's a street.

OTTO. No sign of the black one but they may have switched vehicles. Although they probably think we're both in the morgue after a deadly collision with a bus.

ELLEN. I didn't even brush that bloody bus.

OTTO. Only because I shouted 'BUS'.

ELLEN. You're very welcome. Even the winner of the Monte Carlo Rally would've lost us after Regent's Park.

OTTO. You did drive very imaginatively.

ELLEN. Well, Mr Katz, in order to achieve my destination,
I must occasionally drive on the wrong side of the road.

OTTO. Now there is a line from a movie. *The Woman Who
Knew Too Much*.

ELLEN. In the film of my life, there better be car chases.

OTTO. You'll have an MI5 file by morning.

ELLEN. Good. You know you're onto something /

OTTO. When someone is chasing you.

ELLEN. Trying to stop you.

OTTO. I like your flat. It's busy.

ELLEN. Give me colour, bleeding from the walls. Do you like
my cups? Hand-painted. And the chairs. Can't stand a plain
chair.

He stands closer. ELLEN *starts coughing.*

Your cologne… my asthma.

OTTO. Sorry.

ELLEN. For a spy, you have a very distinctive scent.

OTTO. I am not a spy.

ELLEN. Said every spy ever.

Beat.

Music!

OTTO. Cole Porter?

ELLEN. Hardly a Soviet staple.

OTTO. I love his way with words. I keep a little book.
Yesterday I learnt… 'to get stuck in.' 'Get bloody well stuck
in.' And… to 'chance it'. 'A good egg.' 'Poppycock.'

ELLEN. Say it again.

OTTO. Poppycock.

ELLEN. You know what I like about you?

OTTO. My ridiculousness?

ELLEN. A ridiculous man isn't chased, at that speed, by Military Intelligence. I like people so serious they don't need to be serious. People who act like, any minute, they might die.

OTTO. Do you want to chance it with my cologne?

ELLEN *steps closer, struggles to breathe for a second, takes a deep breath and then kisses him.*

On the gramophone Al Bowlly sings Cole Porter's 'How Could We Be Wrong' accompanied by Ray Noble and his Orchestra. They dance together. It is the kind of night that rarely gets repeated.

Scene Five

Outside her flat in Bloomsbury. ELLEN *is maintaining her motorcar (her beloved Austin 7).*

Enter HERBERT.

HERBERT. What are you doing?

ELLEN. Replenishing my crankcase, what does it look like?

HERBERT. Stop gallivanting with Reds.

ELLEN. So, you're anti-anti-fascism?

HERBERT. It's a cynical plot. By rebranding as 'anti-fascists' they're setting themselves up as the 'good guys', thereby upping their recruitment chances.

ELLEN. What bit of 'The Relief Committee for the Victims of German Fascism' do you not agree with, Herbert?

HERBERT. The bit where all the funds get sent to Moscow.

ELLEN. Dipstick.

HERBERT. Pardon?

ELLEN. Pass me the dipstick so I may check the oil. You're obsessed with infiltration.

HERBERT. What do you think is happening in Russia right now? You think everyone's ploughing the land together with big smiles on their faces?

ELLEN. They're doing what OUR PARTY should be doing. I have a dent right down my lifeline. Collection-bucket stigmata.

HERBERT. I can smell the drink off you.

ELLEN. Don't smell me then.

She offers HERBERT *a cigarette.*

HERBERT. You're… glowing. Your eyes are all sparkling.

ELLEN. Why thank you.

HERBERT. It's sinister. You're on the turn. They've got their teeth in your neck. By next week you'll be wandering in a languor through a poppy field in a wet nightie waving a flag.

ELLEN. Communists are human beings, Herbert.

HERBERT. No, they're operatives. Operating.

ELLEN. We mainly listen to music and drink cocktails.

HERBERT. Exactly. They are seducing you with the romance of their cause. You think their martinis aren't manipulative?

ELLEN. Well God forbid there should be any romance in a cause, hey Herbert.

HERBERT. Politics isn't about charm.

ELLEN. Certainly not in your case.

HERBERT. The Labour Party stands for the democratic advance towards socialism. The British Communist Party believes in class war. Where are you, in that?

ELLEN. It's a spectrum.

HERBERT. Are you a Communist?

ELLEN. I'm on the side of the people.

HERBERT. Fighting for democracy and revolution does not double your chances. A person who cannot draw a line is a person with no values.

ELLEN. I have values.

HERBERT. You have *all* of them.

ELLEN. Our first constituency is the world, as contradictory as it may be.

HERBERT. You are not the MP for the world, Ellen.

ELLEN. Until I win a seat, I am.

HERBERT. So, this is about you? Needing a purpose?

ELLEN. Oh! Like I'm flower-arranging: 'busying myself' by taking on Hitler.

HERBERT. Is *that* what you're doing?

Enter OTTO.

OTTO. Morning.

OTTO *and* ELLEN *get in the car.* OTTO *hands* ELLEN *a manuscript.*

Give this book to your publishing house.

ELLEN. What is it?

OTTO. The untold truth about the horrors of the Third Reich, endorsed by Albert Einstein himself.

HERBERT. Ellen.

ELLEN. Bye, bye. Mind your fingers.

ELLEN *slams the door and starts the engine.*

ACT TWO

Scene One

Essex Hall. Fundraising meeting for 'The Relief Committee for the Victims of German Fascism'.

The hall is packed.

ELLEN. I am certain, as kind and conscientious people, you have been to many fundraisers before: you sit, listen, think 'that sounds perfectly dreadful', tinkle a coin into the can. This is not that kind of evening. I am not here to play. Showing up is not enough. I cannot give your attendance to the sixty thousand people in concentration camps. I cannot give your attendance to the Jews being persecuted and tortured and hounded out of their businesses. I cannot give your attendance to the refugee children crying without their mothers. This bucket is not a begging bowl – it is your opportunity to exist.

Beat.

We will be here for the next hour, help yourself to hot punch, buy a book – *THE BROWN BOOK OF HITLER TERROR*, endorsed by Albert Einstein himself, if you don't believe me, believe Einstein.

Afterwards, at the book stand...

How was I? Was it alright?

ISABEL. It was bit much.

ELLEN. It worked, didn't it? They were jostling in the aisles, perched on windowsills, it was like an Ivor Novello concert.

ISABEL. You can switch to your indoor voice now.

ELLEN (*in a baby voice*). I'm sorry.

Enter OTTO.

OTTO. Enchanting. Devastating. Brought the house down. Bravo. I can see where you get your aliases from.

ELLEN. Aliases?

OTTO. Your many identities. The Mighty Atom. The Fiery Particle. Elfin Fury.

ELLEN. They're nicknames, not aliases.

OTTO. Hmm. We need to make more of the Einstein endorsement. We have not sold enough books.

ELLEN. Of course.

Exit OTTO.

Isabel.

ISABEL. What?

ELLEN. Remind me how this money reaches the victims? The German resistance?

ISABEL *counts their takings.*

It doesn't... it doesn't *all* just go to Moscow, does it?

ISABEL. Ellen. A wise man once said, 'Light yourself on fire and people will come for miles to watch you burn.' You were aflame on that stage. Who in their right mind would light herself on fire without knowing exactly what it was she was fighting for?

ELLEN. I do know.

ISABEL. I know you know. You do coins, I'll do notes.

Enter OTTO.

OTTO. Just to say, we have had a slight hitch.

ELLEN. A hitch?

OTTO. Could you fly to Belgium?

ELLEN. Why? When?

OTTO. Right now.

Scene Two

Autumn 1933. Belgium. EINSTEIN*'s villa.*

A SECURITY MAN *is standing by the door.*

ELLEN. I am so, so, so, so, so, so, sorry, Professor Einstein.
   Honestly the moment I realised what had happened, all the
   blood in my veins turned to ice, crimson ice, frozen claret,
   honestly, I went into shock from the guilt of it, palpitations,
   the lot, and immediately I said to myself I said, 'Ellen, you
   must get on a plane to Belgium right this second and
   apologise to the great man in person. Face to face.'

EINSTEIN. Who are you?

ELLEN. My name is Ellen Wilkinson /...

EINSTEIN. What are you doing here?

ELLEN. ...politician, raconteur... and also the secretary for
   'The Relief Committee for the Victims of German Fascism'.

EINSTEIN. That committee almost killed me.

ELLEN. I chastised myself, I said this is beyond the realm of
   normal human error –

EINSTEIN. What do you want?

ELLEN. Two things. One: To apologise from the bottom of my
   heart. Two: To persuade you not to resign as our honorary
   president.

EINSTEIN. Surely the latter motive dilutes the sincerity of the
   first?

ELLEN. Not at all. I want both equally. As I was saying –
   I COULD NOT BELIEVE, in my attempts to thwart Hitler,
   I accidentally endangered the life of the most influential
   Jewish man of our times. Honestly, I am tempted to lie
   prostrate on the floor at your feet...

EINSTEIN. That might be a little alarming.

   Beat.

ELLEN. Lovely carpet.

EINSTEIN. Thank you.

ELLEN. Is this your house?

EINSTEIN. When you're fleeing for your life, my dear, it generally makes more sense to rent.

ELLEN. What happened was, my anti-fascist colleagues approached me with this incredible manuscript. The testimonies travelled via the resistance, written on skin, bandages, soles of shoes, hidden inside the dresses of dolls. Finally, I thought, a book that tells the truth about Nazi atrocities…

EINSTEIN. It also contains a bizarre sequence about a homosexual storm-trooper conspiracy.

ELLEN. There are elements of propaganda, yes. But I'd rather publish a book with ninety per cent truth and ten per cent propaganda than publish no book at all.

EINSTEIN. Miss Wilkinson.

ELLEN. Yes.

EINSTEIN. There is no such thing as ninety per cent truth.

ELLEN. Right. You'd know. Good maths. I'm so sorry.

EINSTEIN *passes her a box of tissues.*

'Einstein passed me a tissue.' Something to tell the grandchildren. 'Einstein once passed me a box of tissues.'

EINSTEIN. You have children?

ELLEN. Oh, no, I was just saying things. Where would I keep them? I'd have to carry them around in my handbag.

EINSTEIN. The Communists sent you for a reason.

ELLEN. Yes, in order to /

EINSTEIN. No, they specifically sent *you* to apologise to me. If they came, they'd have to lie.

ELLEN. I honestly didn't know you hadn't agreed to the endorsement.

EINSTEIN. I believe you.

Beat.

Did it not occur to you to ask, *should* a Jewish man risk associating his name with a publication guaranteed to enrage the Nazis?

ELLEN. I suppose... I didn't think of you that way.

EINSTEIN. As a Jew?

ELLEN. I thought – 'Einstein'. The Extraordinary Albert Einstein.

EINSTEIN. No Jew is exempt from anti-Semitism.

ELLEN. No.

EINSTEIN. If this experience has taught me anything, it's that 'extraordinariness' is but temporarily permitted of us.

ELLEN *doesn't understand.*

If the box you tick on a form is not considered equal by ordinary society, Miss Wilkinson, it does not matter how extraordinary you are. Any vision you may have of yourself and your own innate qualities is at best a galvanising dream, and at worst, a delusion likely to get you killed by the same men who once permitted your extraordinary work.

EINSTEIN *passes* ELLEN *an ashtray.*

Einstein just passed you an ashtray.

ELLEN (*putting out her hand*). So, you won't resign? You'll forgive me? We can be friends?

EINSTEIN (*shaking it*). Are you leaving?

ELLEN. It's just... ûm... my father's dying.

Exit ELLEN, *running.*

Scene Three

ELLEN*'s childhood home in Manchester.*

There is a tin bath in the corner. A needlepoint sermon on the wall. A threadbare ironing board. A few items of clothing hung in an old wardrobe. Through ELLEN*'s eyes at least, everything has a grey tinge.*

ANNIE *and* ELLEN *have just left their father's bedroom.*

ANNIE. I need to call the doctor.

ELLEN. It's a bit late now.

ANNIE. We need a certificate, for the medical... cause of...

ELLEN. The cause was you.

   Beat.

ANNIE. Ellen.

ELLEN. How could you do that?

ANNIE. What?

ELLEN. What gave you the right?

ANNIE. I don't know what you mean.

ELLEN. You opened your mouth, your little whispery gentle angelic surrendering mouth, and you ordered him to give up.

ANNIE. Ellen, you're upset and it's coming out in a strange way /

ELLEN. You practically summoned a troop of angels.

ANNIE. What?

ELLEN. 'It's time to go now, Dad, let yourself go, we love you, you can go.'

ANNIE. What's wrong with that?

ELLEN. You did not speak for me.

ANNIE. Ellen, please...

ELLEN. I tried to reverse your 'instruction'.

ANNIE. Instruction?

ELLEN. I gripped his hand and… Do not touch that phone. If I can just pin-point – so I held his hand, I said – I can't remember – but I galvanised him, he resuscitated, the breathing got stronger…

ANNIE. It wasn't that sort of breath.

ELLEN. You're not a qualified nurse.

ANNIE. Ellen, please, you're making this so much worse.

ELLEN. I am? 'Making it worse.' Right, I see. I see the words you're throwing around. Acceptance. Surrender.

ANNIE. I haven't said either of those / words.

ELLEN. This is exactly the argument against any sort of idealism.

ANNIE. What?

ELLEN. When I arrived, his head was turned to the wall, his lips were all chapped.

ANNIE. The doctor said nil by mouth, just dab his lips with a moist cloth /

ELLEN. Human beings need water. For God's sake, woman.

ANNIE. Please stop /

ELLEN. But when he heard *my* voice, his spirit stirred, he rose /

ANNIE. He didn't rise.

ELLEN. It was *definite*, he knew it was me, and he made a sound, he was alive again. Then twelve hours later, you lean forward and snip his cord.

ANNIE. Ellen, this is unacceptable. I didn't 'snip' anything /

ELLEN. Is it a coincidence that he died two minutes later? Is that a coincidence?

ANNIE. No.

ELLEN. No.

ANNIE. He needed to go, but he was holding on.

ELLEN. Because of me.

ANNIE. Yes.

ELLEN. So, if you hadn't said that...

ANNIE. He might have hung on, in terrible pain, for another few hours.

ELLEN. Or turned a corner. There might've been...

ANNIE. A miracle?

Beat.

He needed permission.

ELLEN. 'Permission.'

ANNIE. Have mercy, Ellen.

ELLEN. He was not a quitter. This was his mantra... THIS:

ELLEN *takes the needle-sampler down from the wall.*

'Do all the good you can,
By all the means you can,
In all the ways you can,
In all the places you can,
At all the times you can,
To all the people you can,
As long as ever you can.'

ANNIE. Death has nothing to do with / quitting

ELLEN. He wasn't finished, I needed to thank him...

ANNIE. You did.

ELLEN. Not enough, I didn't thank him enough.

ANNIE. Oh, Ellen.

ELLEN. And you took that from me.

ANNIE. I'm making tea then I'm calling /

ELLEN. You and Mum never wanted me to get better.

Beat.

If you'd had your way, I'd have had Scarlet Fever for the rest of my life, I'd have died in that bed, suffocated in blankets and bonnets and fuss. My dad never said, 'You can't.' He never said, 'Give up.'

ANNIE. You are being so cruel.

ELLEN. He said, 'Let's live. Let's go to a lecture on Darwin, let's play chess, what is *your* opinion on this book...'

ANNIE. Good for you.

ELLEN. You will never understand our bond.

ANNIE. No, I won't.

ELLEN. No.

ANNIE. Because I didn't have any of that. Annie can look after Mum. Annie doesn't need to finish school. Annie can have a sewing machine for Christmas and make clothes for Ellen to be interesting in. If someone had taken *me* to lectures...

ELLEN. He didn't take you, he took *me*, he saw something in *me*...

ANNIE. Alright.

ELLEN. Something that does not die.

ANNIE. Well, he's dead. So. And I nursed him, and you didn't. You rocked up at the last minute and took a bow. And now *this* is what I'll remember. So thanks.

ELLEN. 'It's time to go now.' Pathetic. Scandalous.

ANNIE. It's a perfectly kind, normal thing to say to...

ELLEN. Kind. Normal.

ANNIE. ...someone you love /

ELLEN. If someone had said that to me, I would've kicked off my blankets and slapped them in the face.

ANNIE. Week after week, I fed him, washed him /

ELLEN. Exactly. You had all that time.

ANNIE. Read to him, sang to him /

ELLEN. I'm sorry I'm not that kind of woman, I'm sorry I'm not a nursemaid, I'm sorry I don't simper and give up and whisper codswallop about letting go, I'm sorry I fight, I'm sorry I'm independent, I'm sorry I've got a job. Look at this place. What chance did he have? It's all grey, death dusted everywhere. Even the leaves are covered in soot. No wonder I've got asthma, no wonder I couldn't breathe, you were always trying to keep me down, that was the man – the only man – who ever fully believed in me.

ANNIE. I believe / in you

ELLEN. I hate your sewing machine. Clicking away, tick-tock, if you had your way we'd both be spinster sisters in matching marigold gloves, kneading grey dough, taking it in turns to have asthma attacks, you wanted him to die because you – you – you – you – all you women are like that, no grit, no resilience, just nurse the world as it dies and dab its mouth and don't give it water and don't rise up, it's inevitable, it's NOT inevitable, you cowardly weak little sap /

ANNIE *slaps* ELLEN *in the face.*

ANNIE. I'm putting the kettle on and then I'm phoning. You're feeling guilty. Because you weren't here.

ELLEN. I'm here now. Here I am. Back here. With the ironing board. And the old tin bath…

ELLEN *stands up and gathers her things.*

Do you need money for the…? Whatever you need…

ANNIE. I need you.

ELLEN. I'm sorry for shouting, I don't know why I… But I have to work, I'm afraid… I need to be /

ANNIE. Somewhere else? Anywhere else?

ELLEN. I love you.

Exit ELLEN, *running.*

ANNIE *phones the doctor.*

Scene Four

Jarrow. November 1935.

ELLEN *is wearing her red rosette, alongside the other candidates.*

ANNOUNCER. William George Pearson. Conservative Party, seventeen thousand, nine hundred and seventy-four.

A decent amount of applause.

Ellen Cicely Wilkinson. Labour Party. Twenty thousand, three hundred and twenty-four.

Cheers.

WILLIAM PEARSON (*to* ELLEN). Congratulations. You've won... eighty per cent unemployment. Jarrow doesn't need an MP it needs a bloody miracle.

Scene Five

Constituent Surgery. September 1936.

A sign saying: 'APPLICANTS FOR THE JARROW MARCH.'

DAVID *has just received news from the doctor, meaning he won't be able to march.*

ELLEN. I'm so sorry, David.

DAVID *takes a ten-inch key from around his neck. It's a big brass 'Good Luck' key to commemorate a 21st birthday.*

DAVID. Do you like my key?

ELLEN. Twenty-one? Happy birthday.

DAVID. Aye. Thanks. Do I look it? Me da made this for me thirty years ago. For our twenty-first birthdays, the metal workers would cut ten-inch keys from the sheets of brass, then smuggle them out past the gateman. Like a key for a giant's house. This is my reminder.

ELLEN. Of your dad?

DAVID. Soppy bollocks. Of our ships. Here's a bit of HMS
Lord Nelson. She fought off the Ottomans, never sustained
a single casualty, she were that strong: a stone cannonball
landed on her deck and the flagman kept it as a souvenir: that
were his, this is mine.

ELLEN. You won the war for us.

Beat.

DAVID (*looking at the key*). Strange thing, isn't it? So grand.
But nowt you can do with it.

ELLEN. Do you want a copy of the doctor's report?

DAVID *doesn't*.

I'm sorry.

DAVID. You've said.

ELLEN. But I know how much you wanted to march.

DAVID. I've never even heard of…

ELLEN. Asbestosis.

DAVID. It's my breathing.

ELLEN. Basically.

DAVID. They murdered my town but I can't even protest
because the work I did – FOR THEM – made us too sick to
march. How's that fair?

ELLEN. It's not.

DAVID. Let us die on the road.

ELLEN. What?

DAVID. If I'm going to die anyway, let us die marching.

ELLEN. Top story in *The Times*: 'Ill man exploited for political
means.'

DAVID. Then I won't die. I'll get stronger.

ELLEN. How?

DAVID. Marching'll bring us back to life.

Beat.

What if it's not asbesto-wotsit? What if it's grief? What if my lungs are packing in for lack of hope? A skilled man sold for scrap. It's the stopping what kills you.

ELLEN. I feel that too.

DAVID. Eh?

ELLEN. It's the stopping that kills you.

DAVID. By the time you get back, I'll be dead from… from… powerlessness. Please, ma'am.

ELLEN. Call me Ellen.

DAVID. Soldier on. Stick it out. Mind over matter.

ELLEN. You sound like my dad. Every morning he'd shout 'Lose yourself in action lest you wither in despair!' whilst banging a saucepan with a wooden spoon. He was rather dramatic.

Beat.

Alright. Sod it.

DAVID. Ma'am?

ELLEN. If you can bash a million sheets of tin to build a fleet of ships, you can manage three hundred miles.

DAVID. Little more to it than tin-bashing, but you're saying…

ELLEN. Yes.

DAVID. I can march?

ELLEN. You can march.

DAVID. YES. YES. YES.

DAVID *runs over to her and gives her a massive hug.*

ELLEN. What do doctors know anyway? If the world was run by doctors no one would ever move.

DAVID. You'll not regret this.

ELLEN. If you believe it, I believe it...

DAVID is breathing heavily, clearly not well enough to march.

David /...

DAVID. Don't.

Beat.

On second thoughts. Thanks for the offer. But. My signature will be on the petition carried by the marchers to Westminster and... that's good enough for me.

ELLEN. I respect your decision.

DAVID *(meaning 'oh, I nearly forgot')*. Oh, aye...

DAVID takes the key from around his neck and puts it in ELLEN's hands.

ELLEN. I can't take this.

DAVID. But you're marching to the gates of power...?

Beat.

Gonna need a big key.

Exit DAVID.

ELLEN almost starts to cry. She struggles to breathe. She slaps herself in the face. She lights a cigarette.

ELLEN. Next!

Scene Six

HERBERT*'s office in London. September 1936.*

HERBERT. Hunger marches are associated with Communism.

ELLEN. It's a crusade for work. Are we not the party of the workers any more? Did I miss a memo? The National Executive of the Labour Party won't even lend a penny for a scrap of boot-leather and a box of nails?

Beat.

You are such a hypocrite.

HERBERT. No, no, no, I really really am not, by politician standards. You, on the other hand, *you… you…*

ELLEN. Spit it out.

HERBERT. Call yourself a pacifist…

ELLEN. I am.

HERBERT. Well, you must be. You signed the Manifesto for Peace and Disarmament last week.

ELLEN. Great manifesto.

HERBERT. Yet you are fighting to open a steelworks in your constituency, the main purpose of which will inevitably be munitions?

ELLEN. The men need work.

HERBERT. You justify your hypocrisy by the strength of your emotions?

ELLEN. It's not / hypocrisy.

HERBERT. At the Peace Union Rally you called for intervention in Spain?

ELLEN. If the British Navy won't stop Hitler or Mussolini shipping weapons to Franco then /

HERBERT. We should give guns to the Spanish workers?

ELLEN. To fight *back* against fascism.

HERBERT. It's not that simple.

ELLEN. YES IT IS. Thousands were herded into a bullring in Badajoz, alright, literally herded like cattle, and slaughtered. Children /

HERBERT. Ellen. You do know that you cannot stand for everything?

Beat.

You cannot say 'arm the people' AND sign the peace manifesto? You do know that? Even if you agree with both simultaneously?

Beat.

ELLEN. What's this got to do with Jarrow?

HERBERT. Think. This march will always be politically suspect, Ellen, because *you* are politically suspect.

ELLEN. I... WHY WON'T MY OWN PARTY SUPPORT ME?

HERBERT. I'm not trying to be horrible.

ELLEN. Turn away.

She peels off her stockings and puts on new ones.

HERBERT. They will crush those men, fob them off and send them away with nothing but blisters and broken dreams.

ELLEN. You want me to give up?

HERBERT. I want us to get elected so that towns like Jarrow can thrive again.

ELLEN. It needs to thrive NOW... these men are alive NOW... We need to act NOW...

HERBERT. You are not as powerful as you think you are, Miss Wilkinson. You are not a queen, you are a pawn.

ELLEN. If a pawn marches to the other side of the board, it *becomes* a queen.

HERBERT. Are you going somewhere?

ELLEN. Berlin.

HERBERT. What?

ELLEN. I'm doing a spot of light investigative journalism...

HERBERT. What?

ELLEN....in my spare time.

Exit ELLEN, *running.*

Scene Seven

A cheap hotel room in Berlin.

ELLEN *is pacing, waiting.*

Knock on the door.

ELLEN. Who is it?

OTTO. The Gestapo.

ELLEN *grabs a fork from her room service tray.*

(*In a German accent.*) We have brought sticky cinnamon pastries.

ELLEN *opens the door.*

ELLEN. Not funny.

OTTO. Were you planning to fork me?

ELLEN. In a minute. What's the story?

OTTO. I have missed you.

ELLEN. You're ridiculously late and my editor is calling in ten minutes. What's the tip?

OTTO. Tip?

ELLEN. I've flown all the way here because you said you had a massive story for me... I've got an exclusive all set up in tomorrow's paper and I don't even know what it is yet. I've worn a path in this carpet from pacing, you... you... meat-head.

OTTO. Meat-head. That's good. And also – accurate, I suppose – about everyone. Kiss me.

ELLEN. Tell me.

OTTO. I do have a massive piece of information.

ELLEN. And?

OTTO. Your editor is calling in ten minutes, you say? But, darling, that is six hundred seconds. (*He tucks into the pastries.*) Six hundred whole, juicy, luscious seconds. They glaze these in butter. If I was a German, I would eat these every day. Although, as a Jew, perhaps I would not be allowed in the bakery. I like your stockings. Stockings is 'Strümpfe'. I should like to tear off your Strümpfe with my teeth.

ELLEN. I'm going to chew your Adam's apple with *my* teeth if you don't start /

OTTO. Spilling the beans?

ELLEN. Right.

OTTO. Do you know the origin of that phrase?

ELLEN. Argh.

OTTO. In Ancient Greece –

ELLEN. We don't have time for Ancient Greece.

OTTO. A long, long time ago, in Ancient Greece, electoral votes were cast in beans, black beans for nay, white beans for yay. Such an innocent system. And yet /

ELLEN. I'm going to punch you in the face.

OTTO. Thirty-eight million Germans voted for the Nazis... that is...

ELLEN. A bloody load of beans /

OTTO. Oi! I was building to a poetic finale.

ELLEN. I'll give *you* a poetic finale.

OTTO. What does that mean?

ELLEN. I don't know.

OTTO. Should I take my trousers off?

ELLEN. Otto!

OTTO. Alright. Have you got a pen?

ELLEN. What's the story?!

OTTO. Shhhhhh. The walls have ears.

ELLEN. I've already checked the room.

OTTO. Both our names are on the Gestapo death list. Well, your name and at least three of mine. (*Pointing.*) They could be there right now with stethoscopes pressed to the wall.

ELLEN *slaps herself in the face*.

Don't do that.

ELLEN. I'm seeing spots.

OTTO. Stay here with me tonight.

ELLEN. My flight's in two hours.

OTTO. Oh.

ELLEN. I would say 'I'll sleep when I'm dead' but I'm sure I'll find something to do in the grave... fighting for 'equality for the worms' or... although that'd piss *someone* off... 'What about the woodlice, Ellen? What about the... the... soil? You little dead hypocrite.'

OTTO. Alright.

ELLEN. Go.

OTTO. Wait. First, you must invent a source.

ELLEN. I'm way ahead of you /

OTTO. No one can suspect this information came from my circle.

ELLEN. I heard it from... a fictional Nazi chum.

OTTO. Chum?

ELLEN. Estranged colleague gone bad from my student days…
and right now we're meeting in a quiet café terrace and I'm
pouring schnapps and saying 'Come on Hans, this isn't you'
and he's welling up and leaning forward to tell me… what?
What is it?

OTTO. Hitler is preparing to march on the Rhineland.

ELLEN. Sod off.

OTTO. They have the plans worked out in minute detail. After
the Olympic Games, they will move.

ELLEN. So, it's happening? They're mobilising troops?

OTTO. Re-militarising.

ELLEN. In other words…

OTTO. Germany is, once again, getting ready for war.

ELLEN. That's my exclusive?

OTTO. Told you it was massive.

ELLEN. And who told *you* this?

OTTO. I am the man who knows everyone.

ELLEN. You have Soviet spies in German High Command?

OTTO (*very serious*). Never, ever say that again.

ELLEN. Why I should trust you?

OTTO. It is true.

ELLEN. You lied to me about Einstein.

OTTO. A little lie can serve a greater truth (as you and your
fictional source both know). But this is a cold stone fact.

ELLEN. Stone cold.

Before OTTO *can finish writing 'stone cold fact' in his
notebook,* ELLEN *jumps on him. They start having sex.*

OTTO. I thought your editor was calling?

ELLEN. I've got two minutes.

OTTO. I can last longer than that.

ELLEN. I'm sure but *I'll* be done in two… and then I'll reveal Hitler's military strategy to the press.

OTTO. Shhhh.

ELLEN. Oh, I've been on a death list since I was five years old.

OTTO. What?

ELLEN. The doctors said I wouldn't live yet here I blooming am.

OTTO. I love you.

ELLEN. Save it for your wife. (*Slaps him.*) Congratulations on your wedding by the way, sorry I didn't buy you a crockery set.

OTTO. I can love two people at the same / time

ELLEN. Shut up. This'll be the biggest article I've ever written. Germany is *breaking* the peace treaty. You can't get a clearer warning than that. Surely… surely… surely… now… the world will have to… act.

ELLEN *comes*.

The phone rings.

ELLEN *leaps off* OTTO, *leaving him to sort himself out*.

She answers the phone.

Scene Eight

8 a.m. 5th October 1936. Jarrow Town Hall.

A hundred pairs of worn, recently repaired boots are lined up on the floor.

ELLEN *is inspecting the boots and writing notes on a clipboard whilst simultaneously in the middle of a fierce debate with the representative from the Jarrow Labour Exchange.*

MR ANSLEY. I feel duty-bound to warn you that in similar cases in the past we have disallowed claims to benefit.

ELLEN. You can't cut their dole. It's all they've got.

MR ANSLEY. We may be unable to accept the applicants as 'job-seeking' whilst they are participating in the march.

ELLEN. Their banner says 'Jobs for Jarrow.' It is literally a job-seeking march.

MR ANSLEY. I don't make the rules.

ELLEN. Have I gone through the looking glass?

MR ANSLEY. Pardon?

ELLEN. Am I about to see a rabbit in a waistcoat and a grinning Cheshire cat?

MR ANSLEY. This is standard procedure.

ELLEN. It's insane.

Enter PETE, *a local volunteer.*

PETE. He doesn't want to shave it.

ELLEN. What?

PETE. Father Christmas.

Beat.

The bloke who looks like Father Christmas.

ELLEN. Send him in. Is the coffee cart here?

PETE. Setting up now.

ELLEN (*pointing at a box of waterproof capes*). And start handing those out.

PETE *goes to leave.*

Pete. You need to model it for them.

PETE. What?

ELLEN. Model the cape. Sorry. Like this.

Enter ISABEL. *She starts stocking leaflets.*

They need to roll the cape over their shoulders, bandolier fashion.

PETE. What do you think this is? *Harper's Bazaar*?

ELLEN. Isabel, what are you doing?

ISABEL. Helping.

ELLEN (*to* MR ANSLEY). I'll be with you in one moment. (*To* ISABEL.) Did Otto send you?

ISABEL. This is my heartland, pet. I don't need 'sending'.

ELLEN. I'm trying to coordinate two hundred men right now.

ISABEL. Primed for revolution. The underlying cause of unemployment is capitalism.

ELLEN. I know but can you keep your voice down please and go away?

ELLEN *picks up a pair of old boots. She goes back to* MR ANSLEY.

How old do you think these boots are? Five years? Ten? Twenty?

MR ANSLEY. I couldn't say.

ELLEN. Our cobbler did an overnight job so they might last till – optimistically – Ripon. Then they'll have to be re-repaired. Why would a man choose to walk two hundred and ninety-one miles in leaky boots by way of a holiday?

MR ANSLEY. No one is suggesting they are holidaying, Miss Wilkinson.

ELLEN. They are marching for work.

Exit ISABEL.

MR ANSLEY. In order to be judged as seeking work, the men must remain in the town in which they are asking for work.

ELLEN. But there's no work here. That's why they're marching.

MR ANSLEY. No need to take a tone with me.

ELLEN. A tone? A TONE?

Enter MATTHEW.

MATTHEW. The organisers want to deface me.

ELLEN. Hi Matthew. One moment, Mr Ansley, and please forgive me for raising my voice.

MR ANSLEY. You are forgiven.

MATTHEW. They want to deface me so /

ELLEN. I heard you the first time. (*Composes herself.*) Is deface the right word?

MATTHEW. Take my face off with a razor.

ELLEN. We can't look like we're sending a huddle of tramps on a hunger march...

MR ANSLEY *tuts*.

Their cynicism not mine, Mr Ansley. Your facial hair is incredibly handsome, Matthew, you look like – (*Can't think of anyone.*) a handsome movie star with a beard... but we've had to set a general policy of clean-shaven-ness so as to avoid some men – not you, obviously – arriving in a bedraggled state. Please. The mayor will be here soon and then we're marching to Christ Church for a short service from the bishop.

MATTHEW. I've had this beard for twenty years.

ELLEN. Please, for me. Shave for me.

MATTHEW. That is a very odd thing to say, miss.

ELLEN (*to* MR ANSLEY). When would you cut it?

MR ANSLEY (*momentarily confused by all the talk about beards*). Cut what?

ELLEN. Their dole.

MR ANSLEY. Should you perhaps have checked this earlier?

Beat.

Any time subsequent to their departure.

ELLEN. Tomorrow? And the march takes twenty-six days. So, their wives and children will *starve* for a month while they're away?

MR ANSLEY. It's not too late to cancel.

Enter ISABEL, *carrying placards: 'Build the United Front' and 'Send Medical Aid to Spain'.*

ELLEN. Those placards are not ours. This is the town's march, it's about everyone.

ISABEL. Exactly. *Everyone.*

ELLEN (*to* MR ANSLEY). May I ask your first name?

MR ANSLEY. Mr Harold Ansley. Of the Jarrow Labour Exchange.

ELLEN. Do you ever feel like a spy, Harold?

MR ANSLEY. I beg your pardon?

ELLEN. A double life. Walking in your suit through the derelict streets.

MR ANSLEY. I don't follow.

ELLEN. In one of the most disadvantaged and stagnant towns in England, your job is one hundred per cent secure *because*, Harold, eighty per cent of your hometown don't have one.

MR ANSLEY. That is not my fault.

ELLEN. No. It is your burden. What a cruel irony for a man to live with. That must be very hard.

Beat.

MATTHEW. What if I just trim it?

ELLEN. MATTHEW. JESUS. Shave it off or sling your hook.

MATTHEW. But...

ELLEN. Unemployed men cannot *look* unemployed or else no one believes them capable of *being* employed /

MATTHEW. I don't understand.

ELLEN. Neither do I. (*To* MR ANSLEY.) How about... I call you every single day on behalf of every single man?

MR ANSLEY. You can't change the rules, Miss Wilkinson, simply by... by...

ELLEN. By what?

MR ANSLEY. Your own powers of persuasion.

ELLEN. In Ferryhill, I will call you. In Darlington, I will call you. In Northallerton, I will call you. In Ripon. Et cetera. They'll be kept in constant touch with the exchange and any potential employers. If a job is found – say a steelworks springs up in our absence – I will personally pay for trains so they may punch in the very next day. You cannot get fairer than that.

Beat.

MR ANSLEY. I will ask my manager.

ELLEN. Thank you, thank you, thank you.

MR ANSLEY. I can't make any promises.

ELLEN. I think you just did, Harry.

Exit MR ANSLEY.

(*To herself.*) Alright, that's fine, that'll be fine.

Enter DAVID, *holding a pair of boots.*

David. Chrissake, GO HOME AND REST!

ISABEL *brings in more placards: 'MILK FOR SPAIN FUND' and 'MUST THEY STARVE?' and 'BUY SPAIN MILK TOKENS AT YOUR CO-OP STORE'.*

ISABEL. You don't think children need milk?

ELLEN. Isabel.

ISABEL. What happened to 'fighting for everything you believe'?

ELLEN. This isn't about propaganda, Isabel. It's a mission with a purpose.

ISABEL. What purpose?

ELLEN. You know 'what'.

ISABEL. Oh God. You actually think that might happen? I'm sorry, I thought you were clever. I thought this was a hunger march to drum up necessary revolutionary zeal. But, no, you actually think the prime minister will meet with your marchers and listen.

ELLEN. It's not a hunger march /

ISABEL. It is, love, straight out of the Soviet playbook, and yet you're marching to parliament to beg the ruling classes for reform? You do see how that doesn't make sense?

ELLEN. The government needs to be informed about Jarrow's plight /

ISABEL. Oh. I see. Informed. They just need to be *informed* and then they'll help? Like we *informed* them about Hitler's advance on the Rhineland? Like we *informed* them about Nazi atrocities? Like we *informed* them about the concentration camps and they've totally jumped into action?

Beat.

ELLEN. You're right. But this is different.

ISABEL. Different how?

ELLEN. This march is about *dramatising* the information, into an unforgettable human event that will visually, physically, poetically, once and for all, force the entire country to truly *understand*.

Beat.

ISABEL. You're a bit muddled you, aren't you?

ELLEN. Muddled?

ISABEL. For an outsider, you've got a helluva lot of faith in the system. The problem isn't that they don't understand, pet, it's that they *do* understand, they just don't care.

Beat.

Good luck.

Exit ISABEL.

DAVID. I'm here to donate.

ELLEN. What?

DAVID. Donate.

ELLEN. Huh?

DAVID. If I can't march in them, I want someone to march in them.

ELLEN. I'm sorry for shouting.

DAVID. You should hear my wife. She can make the windows rattle. No, she can, we have windows like paper, they don't fit right in the frames.

ELLEN. I'll contact the Housing Association. I will. You need proper windows.

Beat.

David. Am I making a mistake?

DAVID. With what?

ELLEN. All this.

DAVID. What??

ELLEN. But what if I fail you?

Beat.

DAVID. With respect, ma'am, this march began years before you got here…

DAVID *leads her out of the town hall*

…it's just taken us this long to get to the start.

The men are all lined up, ready to go, banners held high. It is a deeply impressive and poignant sight.

DAVID *hands his boots to (a freshly-shaven)* MATTHEW *who thanks him and puts them on.*

Scene Nine

The Jarrow March.

A great folk movement.

Under their main banner – 'Jarrow Crusade' – the men march on their four hundred feet. Spirits high, with harmonicas and kettledrums...

It looks like a victory.

Song.

> On our last legs
> we're thumping through the rain and sleet,
> on our last legs
> we're coming on our own two feet,
> on our last legs
> we're drumming to a blistered beat,
> it's the last leg, lads,
> from here to Downing Street
>
> On our last legs
> we're marching to the big front door
> with our last chance
> petition for the chamber floor,
> in the long lost
> tradition of give-'em-what-for,
> it's the last leg, lads,
> from here to Westminster
>
> And we're not there yet
> but we're dressed for the weather

and we're not there yet
but we're patching up our leather
though the miles roll out forever
we'll be ten abreast together,
if you don't ask
you don't get
and we're getting there,
step by step by step...

On our last legs
we're gonna make the bastards see,
may our last word
communicate our final plea:
let this last breath
resuscitate our industry!
It's the last leg, lads,
from here to history

And we're not there yet
but we're dressed for the weather
and we're not there yet
but we're patching up our leather
though the miles roll out forever
we'll be ten abreast together,
if you don't ask
you don't get
and we're getting there,
step by step by step...

ELLEN *gasps for breath*.

Interval.

ACT THREE

Scene One

Madrid, Spain, April 1937.

A huge explosion. ELLEN *is behind the wheel of a car. There is blood, dust and debris all over the windscreen. Shouting and commotion as the aftermath is dealt with.*

Instinctively, ELLEN *turns on the windscreen wipers. She switches them off in horror. She leaps out and starts apologising to the blood.*

ELLEN. Forgive me, that was disrespectful, here, let me...

She uses her scarf as a cloth.

Gently, gently, sorry, I... You're still warm.

She stares down at the bloody scarf and talks to it like a person.

My name's Ellen and I'm sorry it's not a nicer scarf and I'm sorry that I couldn't stop that bomb from going off and I'm sorry that I don't know your name. Juan? Miguel? They're already scooping you up... Were you just walking home or...

Beat.

I hate those new pine coffins. Manufactured in bulk, it's sinister...

Beat.

I resigned from the Pacifist Society. I know they are right. But one cannot 'resolve the issue by peaceful debate' once they're scraping you off a car...

She picks a bit of brain off her blouse.

(*To the bit of brain.*) Spain will unite the Left. I feel it. Every dreamer in the western world has travelled here to join your revolution: '¡No pasarán, Pasaremos!' The fascists shall not pass, but we will.

Beat.

Together. We will.

Scene Two

The bar of the Hotel Florida. 3 a.m. A grandiose hotel on the Plaza de Callao. All the reporters and writers are staying here. It's an odd mix of luxury and war.

ERNEST HEMINGWAY, OTTO KATZ *and* ELLEN *are on their tenth bottle of wine.*

HEMINGWAY. Everything tastes good, doesn't it? I never thought I'd spunk over a tinned sardine. (*Swatting a mosquito.*) Little mozzie sons of bitches drinking for free. No food queues for them. Your little lady's very quiet.

OTTO. She saw a man die today.

HEMINGWAY. Lucky you. Use the rage, baby. We're here to fight.

ELLEN. I thought you were here to film a documentary?

HEMINGWAY. *The Spanish Earth* written and narrated by Ernest Hemingway. An anti-fascist immortalisation of the collective dignity of the humble Spaniard. And after that, I'll write a killer novel.

OTTO. Then I'll recruit him for the KGB.

HEMINGWAY. This guy!

ELLEN (*under her breath*). Is being an idiot.

OTTO. She's depressed. She organised a hunger march in England and it failed. Two hundred men shoved into the tearoom at Westminster then bundled on a train straight back to shitsville. Would be funny if it weren't so sad.

ELLEN. It is not remotely funny.

OTTO. But it was a heroic failure.

ELLEN. I don't want to talk about it.

OTTO. 'The march failed because of me. They lost their dole because of me. The world is doomed because of me.' Our brand is failure, baby. We fail, fail, fail until the day we win.

ELLEN. Don't call me baby.

Beat.

But yes. To hell with reform. (*Raising her glass.*) Long live the revolution /

HEMINGWAY. Fuck, this wine tastes like kidney failure.

OTTO. Let me open a fresh bottle of Sovetskoye Shampanskoye.

HEMINGWAY. Whatty what?

OTTO. Now that the Soviet Union is developing, our wine-makers have devised a new 'bubbly for the people', fizz without the fascism.

HEMINGWAY (*enjoying pronouncing it*). Sovetskoye Shampanskoye.

OTTO (*to* HEMINGWAY, *opening the bottle*). Ooh so, funny story. I was dining with the playwright Lillian Hellman in Pareee – when who sweeps over to our table but Marlene Dietrich? It had been years since we saw each other...

HEMINGWAY. Now *that* I would do.

OTTO. Did you know she was my first wife?

ELLEN. Eh?

HEMINGWAY. Marlene fucking Dietrich was your wife?

OTTO. It's true. Go and check the registry in Teplice if you don't believe me.

HEMINGWAY. What was she like?

OTTO *pops the cork and pours.*

OTTO. This was back in my theatre years in Zurich /

HEMINGWAY. I don't give a fuck about that, I mean what was she *like*?

OTTO. An absolute animal.

HEMINGWAY *takes a swig*.

HEMINGWAY. That's Moët.

OTTO. Uncanny, no? In Siberia, this stuff is cheaper than beer.

HEMINGWAY (*impressed*). Hell, well, it sure tastes like Moët.

ELLEN. I'm going to bed. Marlene Dietrich was *not* your wife.

Enter JOHN DOS PASSOS, *drunk*.

HEMINGWAY. Here he is. John Dos Passos, the *second* best American novelist...

ELLEN *pauses on her way out*.

...and a tight bastard. Two chocolate bars and an orange. That's all he brought. No pâté. No sardines.

DOS PASSOS. My friend is dead and you wanna talk about pâté?

HEMINGWAY. Not this again, John... move on...

DOS PASSOS. Move on?

HEMINGWAY. Your friend deserves to be dead.

DOS PASSOS *runs at* HEMINGWAY. HEMINGWAY *stands. They square up*.

OTTO. Go. Just men being men.

ELLEN *doesn't go*.

DOS PASSOS. He wasn't a traitor.

HEMINGWAY. A sneaky secret Franco-loving filthy fifth column...

DOS PASSOS. I'll bite your fucking ear off.

DOS PASSOS *lunges at* HEMINGWAY *and bites his ear*.

HEMINGWAY. ARGHGH.

They start circling each other like drunken boxers.

DOS PASSOS. José was a life-long socialist.

HEMINGWAY *punches.* DOS PASSOS *ducks.*

HEMINGWAY. Why would the Left murder their own,
dumbass?

DOS PASSOS (*referring to* OTTO). Ask the head executioner.

OTTO. We had reason to believe your friend was working for
the enemy.

HEMINGWAY. YEAH.

DOS PASSOS. With what proof?

OTTO.... after a long and careful trial in which all the charges
were confirmed.

DOS PASSOS. You're making shit up.

HEMINGWAY. The traitorous fascist charges.

DOS PASSOS. Lies. He was a poet.

HEMINGWAY. A traitor poet.

DOS PASSOS. This isn't even your war.

HEMINGWAY. I'm on the side of the Left.

DOS PASSOS. Which left? His left or my left?

ELLEN observes.

HEMINGWAY. I'm here to save Madrid.

HEMINGWAY *picks up the bottle of 'Sovetskoye
Shampanskoye' to take to bed with him.*

Some guys just don't know what they're fighting for.

Exit HEMINGWAY.

DOS PASSOS. DON'T YOU WALK AWAY FROM... (*Breaks
down.*)

Beat.

ELLEN. Otto, what have you done to his friend?

OTTO. My name is André Simone and I have done nothing.

DOS PASSOS. Who are you? Are you a journalist?

ELLEN. No, well sometimes, but /

OTTO. She is just a backbencher for a little English party.

ELLEN. Excuse me?

OTTO. Trust me. This is bigger than you.

DOS PASSOS (*to* ELLEN). Tell your government, this is ALL a smoke screen.

OTTO. Go to bed, John.

DOS PASSOS. They're here to fight fascism, sure, they're also here to murder socialists and Trotskyites, all the 'wrong leftists'... whilst looting all the fucking Spanish gold...

OTTO. John. Bed.

DOS PASSOS. The Russians aren't here to assist the uprising they're here to crush it.

OTTO. Has he even read our manifesto?

DOS PASSOS. Are you kidding? If Karl Marx were alive, he'd be branded a fascist traitor and executed 'after a thorough trial'. THE COMMUNISTS DON'T WANT REVOLUTION. THEY ARE KILLING THE REVOLUTIONARIES.

Suddenly completely sober, OTTO *takes a gun from inside his jacket pocket.*

OTTO. I think we have had enough politics for one night.

Beat.

DOS PASSOS. Whatever it is you're looking for, madam, you're not going to find it here.

Exit DOS PASSOS. OTTO *opens another bottle.*

OTTO. What a racket. Guests are sleeping.

Beat.

Do not believe the conspiracy theories of a grieving man.

Beat.

I love you.

ELLEN. Were you pretending to be drunk?

OTTO. I do not really feel alcohol any more. Water vodka all the same.

ELLEN. Truth lies all the same.

OTTO *changes, his persona drops for a moment.*

OTTO. I do not lie.

ELLEN. You've told me… 'a little lie in service of a greater truth'. But *murdering /*

OTTO. I HAVE NEVER LIED.

Beat.

The facts are not the truth.

ELLEN. What?

OTTO. The Soviet Union is the truth. If we execute you, then you are a traitor. Stalin does not make mistakes.

Enter ISABEL.

ISABEL. Ellen! I need British visas for twenty-five German Communist MPs by the break of dawn. Well, 7 a.m. but dawn sounds better. And… Oh – bleurgh – have I interrupted?

OTTO *switches back to his fun persona.*

OTTO. She is tired, poor thing.

ELLEN. I'm never tired.

OTTO. Wind your neck in.

ELLEN. *What* did you / say

OTTO (*getting out his little black notebook*). Sorry, is this the wrong phrase? I learnt it this morning.

ISABEL. Keep your wig on?

OTTO. Miss Wilkinson's hair is irrefutably her own. Sovetskoye Shampanskoye?

ISABEL. Why not? Wet my whistle.

OTTO. Lovely phrase.

ELLEN (*to both of them*). Don't you – do that.

ISABEL. Do what?

Beat. ELLEN *looks at them both, suddenly deeply unnerved as if they are total strangers.*

ELLEN. Is that a bottle of Moët with the label peeled off?

ISABEL. That would be a very elaborate lie.

ELLEN. Yes.

Beat.

Yes, it would.

Scene Three

ANNIE*'s cottage in Buckinghamshire.*

ANNIE *is going through a particularly bad episode of illness. Her asthma is so bad she can barely talk.*

ELLEN *'cares at speed' for the duration of the scene; e.g. checking* ANNIE*'s temperature, plumping pillows, getting a fresh glass of water, unpacking magazines/chocolates/ oranges, etc.*

ELLEN. Sorry I'm late my plane got hit by lightning. Huge white blue flash and I thought: Annie, we must be buried in the same grave when we die, side by side, agreed?

ANNIE. Hello Ellen. Nice to see you.

ELLEN. The Communists are not my friends.

Beat.

You don't look surprised.

ANNIE *arranges her eyebrows and mouth into a comically surprised expression.*

So, I need a different united front, new connections.

ANNIE. What about... your own party?

ELLEN. I need allies with clout.

ANNIE. That's me out then.

ELLEN. What?

ANNIE. I said that's me out then.

ELLEN. Oh. You'll be up and at 'em soon. Who are the flowers from?

ANNIE. Petula. She's been wonderful /

ELLEN. Where on God's green earth am I going to find honest, media-savvy, non-pacifist fellow *socialists* with enormous clout?

ANNIE *opens her new magazine and holds it up to her face. It is* The Lady's Companion.

I CANNOT FAIL AGAIN! (*Almost breezily.*) The question is, Annie, how do I fight fascism without sacrificing any of my principles?

ANNIE *stares at her, far too ill for this conversation.*

Exit ELLEN, *running.*

Scene Four

March, 1940. WINSTON CHURCHILL*'s office.*

ELLEN (*to herself*). Oh for fuck's sake.

She knocks.

CHURCHILL. Enter. Sit down. Or maybe you should stand, if you sit I shan't be able to see you. You are even shorter up close than from the other side of the house. Surely that cannot make scientific sense. Go on then. Waffle.

ELLEN. I'm sorry?

CHURCHILL. All you backbenchers have been trotting in and waffling, get it out of your system.

Beat.

ELLEN. Shall we begin this again? I'll go out and come in and you can shake my hand as you would a man.

CHURCHILL. This is merely a courtesy.

ELLEN. You asked to see me, Mr Churchill. You would not have done so if you did not understand the value I can bring to your administration. I have never liked you, and yet you are in the historical and unprecedented position of having to form a united government that represents the entire country and for that you need politicians from opposite sides of the political spectrum.

CHURCHILL. What do you mean you don't like me?

ELLEN. I enjoy a droll grump, on a personal level.

CHURCHILL. A droll grump?

ELLEN. May I speak plainly?

CHURCHILL. You mean you're not already?

ELLEN. All I want… is to win.

CHURCHILL. So you do not long for peace negotiations?

ELLEN. You can't cut steel with a rubber knife. And you, sir, are a real, proper, genuine, stainless steel…

CHURCHILL. Bastard?

ELLEN. Whatever gets the job done.

CHURCHILL *laughs*.

CHURCHILL. There could be no reports of you gallivanting
with Soviets in some Soho dive.

ELLEN. My gallivanting days are over.

CHURCHILL. Oh really? And what about agitation? You
cannot encourage strike action when Britain is under attack.

ELLEN (*can't help herself*). Although, striking is a human
right.

CHURCHILL. Not in wartime. Every hour the factories lose is
an hour of surrender to Hitler.

ELLEN. How convenient for the ruling classes that wartime
aligns so perfectly with their interests.

CHURCHILL. See? Things like that. You cannot say things like
that.

ELLEN. I am an Englishwoman. Fighting for England. Same as
you.

CHURCHILL. I'm not a woman.

ELLEN. Clearly, or you wouldn't have campaigned quite so
vigorously against our suffrage.

CHURCHILL *doesn't laugh*.

CHURCHILL. What colour are your eyes?

ELLEN. Brown.

CHURCHILL. Everyone remembers your march. For some
reason, your silly Jarrow 'crusade' has been romantised as
some sort of heroic folk movement.

ELLEN. They *were* heroes.

CHURCHILL. But you'll be in *my* administration. My way.
Not some Geordie miner's way. Not Mrs Peasbody from the
post office's way. Mine.

ELLEN. Understood.

CHURCHILL. You cannot be both the government *and* the opposition.

ELLEN. The only power I wish to oppose is Hitler.

CHURCHILL. Is that true?

Beat.

ELLEN. I cannot turn Britain socialist if she doesn't exist. After we win the war, I will have decades, Mr Churchill, to implement my beliefs. And you will hate me for it. But, yes, right now, I will work for you. So that in twenty years' time, when I am chancellor – or prime minister – you can wave your walking stick at me from the other side of the house.

Beat.

CHURCHILL. Alright, alright, I can use this. Your energy and your, your...

ELLEN. Drive?

CHURCHILL. Your womanliness. And humble background. Manchester, is it? Housewives will listen to you. Mr Morrison thinks you'd be most effective in the Home Office. What do you know about air-raid shelters?

Scene Five

The height of the Blitz.

The Tilbury Shelter in Stepney, in the basement of Whitechapel's huge railway goods terminal on Commercial Road, one of London's largest unofficial public air-raid shelters. Dank, dark, dirty and verminous. It is supposed to cater for 3,000 people — but numbers have now swelled to between 14,000–18,000.

ELLEN *has been sent to inspect the 'Nightmare Arches'. She takes notes.*

MARY. My children are sleeping in straw like horses, my mum's sleeping on a plank of wood.

ELLEN. I understand, but this is not an official shelter.

MARY. I'd say fifteen thousand people makes it official, wouldn't you?

ELLEN. Quite the opposite. And you are under a railway station, which is a military objective.

MARY. Was my cousin's house a military objective?

ELLEN. What's your name?

MARY. Mary.

ELLEN. The government advises surface shelters, Mary.

MARY. London is on fire.

ELLEN. I know it feels / that way

MARY. Would you shelter on the surface of a fire?

ELLEN (*uncomfortable*). It's called a 'dispersal policy'. The Minister of Home Security and all our experts /

MARY. 'Experts.'

ELLEN. Excuse me?

MARY. The government wants to 'disperse' us because they don't want to pay for deep shelters.

ELLEN. That's... that's not the reason.

MARY. If loads of people die in one place, you lot get blamed. But if we all die in our own homes, all over the place – well, that's just bad luck. Our own faults. It's a con.

ELLEN. It's not / a con.

LILY (*shouting from the back*). It's not about keeping us alive, is it?

ELLEN. Pardon?

LILY. Why don't you have a policy about *stopping* us dying?

MARY. Why won't you open the underground?

ELLEN (*gritting her teeth*). The matter is under urgent and active review.

MARY. That's a government phrase.

ELLEN. We're doing all we can.

MARY. There she goes again.

ELLEN (*trying to give her a pamphlet*). The guidelines are clear. Strengthening one's home is the best defence /

MARY. What about the slums? The tenements? It's all very well if you've got a fancy middle-class home.

ELLEN. Do you have an Anderson?

MARY. Don't have a garden.

LILY. I've got one. It's dark, freezing and the rain gets in.

LILY *stands up and comes over to them.*

Is she from the council?

ELLEN. I am the parliamentary secretary for the Minister of Home Security.

MARY. She's that Ellen Wilkinson.

ELLEN. I'm in charge of air-raid shelters.

MARY. I used to like her.

ELLEN. I often say that by the time we have finished this war, we shall be thoroughly trained to run a good one.

Beat.

MARY. Are you making a joke?

Beat.

You're not my friend.

ELLEN. To water-proof your Anderson, you can remove the earth covering and treat the roof with a layer of asphaltic or bitumastic material.

LILY. You what?

MARY. She's a widow not a builder.

ELLEN. Your daughter could help you –

MARY. Oh could I?

ELLEN (*handing over another pamphlet*). Or –

MARY. Is this all you lot are good for?

ELLEN. For a fee of half-a-guinea, a panel of consultants will inspect your house /

MARY. For a fee, is it?

ELLEN. ...and give a written report on the best way /

MARY. They're letting the working classes burn. It's a cull, Mum. A CULL.

ELLEN. Look, I'll give you half-a-guinea.

MARY. You'll give fifteen thousand people half-a-guinea?

ELLEN. I... Mary... I'm working class too.

MARY. Nice coat. (*To* LILY.) She's just like all the rest of them.

LILY. No, love, she's not.

ELLEN. Thank you.

LILY. She's worse.

Beat.

I'd expect this kind of heartlessness from a man. But a woman is supposed to care. You're the opposite of a mother. The Shelter Queen. Tucking thousands of kiddies into filthy, cold cribs while bombs are falling on their heads.

ELLEN. I know you're scared.

LILY. You know nothing, love... about what it means to be me, or her, or anyone down here.

The sound of a huge explosion. LILY *and* MARY *both duck and put their hands over their heads.*

ELLEN *stays standing and looks up, as if – in that moment – willing the entire sky to fall. When she lowers her gaze, she's crying.*

Scene Six

ELLEN *emerges from the underground shelter.*

NEWSPAPER ARTICLE (*voiceover, recording*). 'The *Daily Worker*, 9th October 1940. London burns whilst Ellen Wilkinson, fur-coated and ill-prepared, fails to provide adequate protection... Thousands Dead and Wounded. All hail the Shelter Queen and her Empire of Ash.'

ELLEN *walks to her apartment building in Bloomsbury.*

Smoking is billowing from the bombed-out roof.

Screaming.

Fire-guards are running in and out with buckets.

She sees one of her hand-painted blue chairs poking out from the rubble.

She gets down on her knees and howls.

ACT FOUR

Scene One

HERBERT*'s house. 4 a.m.* ELLEN *is holding a cardboard box full of her salvaged belongings.*

ELLEN. I found a slither of teacup. Is that the right word? Slither?

HERBERT. Sliver. Come in, come in...

ELLEN. Sliver – you're clever – sliver of teacup. And these books. Nice pyjamas. You look like – what's his name? Wee Willie Winkle. Is that right?

HERBERT. I'm so sorry about your flat.

ELLEN. Oh, no, no, don't be, it's a good thing.

HERBERT. How?

ELLEN. Bombs – they don't discriminate. The great leveller. Why should Mary's cousin's house be blasted to smithereens while a government employee gets to keep her lovely little hand-painted... (*Wells up.*)

HERBERT. Don't you have... friends?

ELLEN. Yes. Loads. But we're due to start work in a few hours so...

HERBERT. What about your sister?

ELLEN. She's in Buckinghamshire and it's midnight.

HERBERT. It's 4 a.m.

ELLEN. Is it? (*Shouting up the stairs.*) Go back to sleep, Margaret. It's no one. Just an orphan of the storm.

HERBERT. My wife isn't here. She moved to the country.

ELLEN. Oh.

Beat.

Is that why your sock has a hole in it?

HERBERT. I also have cracker crumbs in my bed.

ELLEN. Wild. While the cat's away...

ELLEN is looking for booze.

HERBERT. Did anyone...? Was anyone at home? In the other flats?

ELLEN. I'm trying not to think right now, Herbert.

HERBERT. All I have to offer is ginger ale.

ELLEN. Are you twelve?

Beat.

Christ.

HERBERT. You drink too much anyway.

ELLEN. I've always found inebriation to be more politically strategic than temperance.

HERBERT. Is that so?

ELLEN. My cocktail parties were legendary. Peter Lorre sipping martinis with Jay Allen... Mahatma Gandhi shaking a White Russian with Willi Münzenberg /

HERBERT. Gandhi doesn't drink.

ELLEN. He drank with me. To think, I sat on my bed, holding this teacup, saying 'Call me crazy, folks, but that Hitler chap is a bad egg.' And tonight, a Nazi bomb incinerated that bed. Bizarre. In other news, the *Daily Worker* calls me 'a thumb-sized parliamentary goon.' Funny word. Goon. I've got a cartoon and everything.

ELLEN takes a pill bottle from her bag.

HERBERT. What's that?

ELLEN. A barbiturate.

HERBERT. We have to be up at six...

ELLEN. If you won't stock brandy what's a girl to do?

HERBERT. It's because... my father was an alcoholic.

ELLEN (*grins*). Look at you, getting personal.

HERBERT *rummages through* ELLEN*'s box of singed books.*

HERBERT. *Searchlight on Spain*, *A Policy for Agriculture*, *Barbarians at the Gate*, *The Principles of Political Economy* and *The Murder at the Vicarage*.

ELLEN. That last one's really political.

HERBERT. You'd make a good Miss Marple.

ELLEN. That reminds me, I lost my lovely little kettle. Bloody hell.

Beat.

HERBERT. Why does Miss Marple remind you of kettles?

ELLEN. My kettle was named Agatha.

Beat.

HERBERT. Do you name all of your appliances?

ELLEN. Kettles play such an active role in our daily lives, Herbert, we use them to sleep, wake, grieve and gossip; they are family members without the appropriate paperwork. So yes, I name my kettle and so should you.

HERBERT. You're a bit mad, aren't you?

ELLEN. Will you cope without your wife? Can you cook?

HERBERT. Beans on toast.

ELLEN. That's the standard male answer, isn't it? 'I can make toast.' Wry chuckle. But it's never true. Put a few blokes in a house-share and within a week they're caramelising onions and cooking beef shins in red wine.

HERBERT. Are you just saying whatever comes into your head?

ELLEN. Generally how conversation works, my friend. That is a gorgeous blanket. It seems incongruous.

HERBERT. Margaret made it.

ELLEN. Wove it?

HERBERT. Yes.

ELLEN. It's very well-weaved. Gosh it even *feels* womanly.

HERBERT. Would you like a cup of tea?

ELLEN. First things first...

ELLEN *fetches his kettle.*

Male or female?

Beat.

Come on.

HERBERT. Male.

ELLEN. Name?

HERBERT. Herbert.

ELLEN. Wow.

HERBERT. Henry. After my dad. He could have done with drinking more tea.

ELLEN. Henry. Yes, he *is* a Henry.

HERBERT. Do you want to name my toaster as well?

ELLEN. Maybe later.

Beat.

HERBERT. You're in shock.

ELLEN. Do I make you feel tall? Objectively speaking, you are short. But I am most definitely shorter. Is that nice?

HERBERT. Are you punishing me for my lack of brandy?

ELLEN. It's nice for me. I can imagine you're a full-sized man.

HERBERT. Full-sized?

ELLEN. And I've grown overnight. Do you respect me, Herbert?

HERBERT. Yes.

ELLEN *moves closer.*

Very much.

ELLEN. Would you be sad if I'd died?

HERBERT. Don't say that.

ELLEN. Would you?

HERBERT. I'd be devastated.

ELLEN. Devastated?

HERBERT. Mournful.

ELLEN moves closer.

ELLEN. It was a direct hit.

HERBERT. Gosh.

ELLEN. If I was at home – in my Morrison shelter – I'd be dead now.

HERBERT. What's your point?

ELLEN. Maybe I did die. Maybe I'm a ghost.

ELLEN moves closer.

HERBERT. You're being strange.

ELLEN. The ghost of Ellen Wilkinson come to haunt you at four in the morning…

ELLEN climbs on top of HERBERT.

HERBERT. What are you doing?

ELLEN. Are my hands cold?

HERBERT. Very.

ELLEN. Can you warm me up?

They kiss. They have sex on top of Margaret's woven blanket.

Scene Two

HERBERT*'s house. 1942.* ELLEN*'s decorations are everywhere: hand-painted blue and orange chairs, hand-painted teacups, colourful throw cushions, Indian rugs, etc.*

HERBERT *is out.* ELLEN *is wearing marigold gloves, manically un-clogging the U-bend in the toilet. Enter* ANNIE, *walking with a cane.*

ELLEN. Are you alright? How are you?

ANNIE. Bit flustered but.

ELLEN. You got the train?

ANNIE. Yes.

ELLEN. How was it?

ANNIE. Hell.

ELLEN. Isn't it just?

ANNIE. What's wrong?

ELLEN. Nothing.

> *Beat.*

ANNIE. Ellen, I'm ill too, and you know I hate leaving the cottage, the cold gets into my lungs, but I'm here because you called and said you needed me.

ELLEN. One second.

ANNIE. What are you...?

ELLEN. I've got an hour off and the U-bend is clogged.

ISABEL. Why are you unclogging another woman's U-bend?

ELLEN. How are *you*? You look troubled, are you troubled?

ANNIE. No. Well, a bit...

ELLEN. Why, what's happened?

ANNIE. Why are you asking me questions about myself?

ELLEN. Oh, Annie...

ELLEN *goes to hug her with her marigold gloves on.*
ANNIE *jumps back.*

Oops. Haha.

ELLEN *takes the gloves off.*

ANNIE. Don't put them in the sink.

ELLEN. OH, I DON'T KNOW DO I? I'm playing house. Why are you troubled?

ANNIE. Petula went back to France.

ELLEN. Who's that?

ANNIE. You never listen to a word I say, do you?

ELLEN. Ah, your cleaner?

ANNIE. Petula was not my cleaner.

ELLEN. Remind me?

ANNIE. It doesn't matter. I accepted, a long time ago, I would always know you better than you know me.

ELLEN. Blooming heck you are sad today.

ANNIE. Why am I here?

ELLEN. Because I've nearly spent my petrol ration for this month. Also…

ANNIE. You needed me?

ELLEN. I thought a trip would do you good. Get out the house. Get some colour in your cheeks.

ANNIE. Your skin is grey.

ELLEN. I'm personifying the London smog.

ANNIE. And you've lost loads of weight.

ELLEN. I haven't.

ANNIE. Go to the doctor's.

ELLEN. They have real victims to attend to.

ANNIE. Get a prescription…

ELLEN. I'm prescribing myself…

ANNIE. What? Sherry?

ELLEN. Adrenaline and asthma cigarettes.

ANNIE. What about sleeping?

ELLEN. I ran out of tablets.

ANNIE. Then go to the /

ELLEN. Stop fussing.

ANNIE. For a socialist, your attitude towards *yourself* is extremely right-wing.

ELLEN. Pardon?

ANNIE. 'Grin and bear it. Put up and shut up.'

ELLEN. There's a war on.

ANNIE. The perfect excuse. You've always felt like a human sacrifice and now it's socially acceptable.

ELLEN. Say what you really mean why don't you?

ANNIE. Being ill is not a weakness.

ELLEN. I'M FINE! I'm washed and dressed, aren't I? I've got decorations up.

ANNIE. In another woman's house.

ELLEN (*coquettishly*). It's a coalition, what can I say?

ANNIE. You called me in tears.

ELLEN. I did?

ANNIE. Sod off, I'm not doing this any more.

ELLEN. What?

ANNIE. I can already tell from your voice you've got some kind of infection. If I spent one second imagining the danger you're in on a daily basis, my heart would simply stop. I have this recurring nightmare about a tattered red kite flying in an electrical storm and I'm tugging at the string but… Pathetic.

ELLEN. Am I the kite?

ANNIE. All I hear is Mum's voice saying 'Where's little Nellie? You're not looking after her.'

ELLEN. I never asked you / to look after me

ANNIE. I'm sorry, Mum, but I have finally realised that I cannot – cannot – hold onto her.

ELLEN. You're not going.

ANNIE. I am.

ELLEN. Please don't go.

ANNIE (*going*). Good luck with your U-bend.

ELLEN. Fine. I…

> ELLEN *starts putting on her fire-watching uniform and helmet.*

> I'm implementing the fire-watching scheme, it's complicated, but (where's my helmet?) women are protesting against compulsory conscription /

ANNIE. Ellen, I am done.

ELLEN. So, I need to set an example, put my money where my mouth is, my stirrup pump where my… spleen is, doesn't work, point is: I'm just the same as anybody else.

> ELLEN *rushes out the door before* ANNIE *can leave her.*

> Close the door when you leave.

ANNIE (*knowing* ELLEN *can't hear*). Don't drive in the blackout, Nellie. It's not safe.

Scene Three

ELLEN *gets in her car.*

She drives in the blackout, with just her sidelights on.

She collides with a lorry.

With her head on the steering wheel, she has a vision of all the desks she's ever sat at, with all the banners she's ever sat beneath – The National Union of Women's Suffrage, The Manchester University Socialist Society, Amalgamated Union of Cooperative Employees, Labour Research Department, The National Council of Labour Colleges, Standing Joint Committee of Industrial Women's Organisations, Trades Union Congress, The National Union of Allied Workers, The Women's Committee for the Relief of the Miners' Wives and Children, The Women's International League for Peace and Freedom, The Relief Committee for the Victims of German Fascism, etc. etc. etc.

Scene Four

ELLEN *wakes up in hospital with bandages around her head.*

ISABEL *is standing over her bed, in a hospital gown.*

ELLEN. ARGHHGGH.

ISABEL. Hello to you too.

ELLEN. What are you doing here?

ISABEL. We're hospital buddies, and you're famous. 'Have you heard… Ellen Wilkinson collided with a lorry.'

ELLEN *feels a terrible wave of pain.*

You've fractured your skull.

ELLEN. How do you know that?

ISABEL. I spoke to your doctor.

ELLEN. How? That's personal.

ISABEL. Come now, you're looking at a woman who chartered illegal planes from Czechoslovakia, I think I can fool one over-worked doctor. And besides, you *are* my sister, of a sort.

Beat. ISABEL *is joking*.

It's written on your chart. I'm not a cartoon villain, Ellen, or do you believe the witch-hunters now? 'Watch out for the Commies. You know they can hang from the rafters like bats? Disguise themselves as bed-pans? Argh, there's one.'

ELLEN (*too hoarse to shout*). Nurse.

ISABEL. You also have acute bronchitis and pneumonia. Why are you scared of me? A bomb burnt my arse, thanks for asking. Quite literally. They had me prostrate under a radium heat lamp for weeks, like an exotic plant. Drying the wounds. Although you'd know all about that. Must be a burns expert by now. Causing enough of them.

ELLEN. Leave me alone.

ISABEL. Sorry, that was mean. But *you're* mean, so mean.

ELLEN. I haven't done anything to you.

ISABEL. So, you and your fella at the Home Office *didn't* ban the *Daily Worker*? You *didn't* silence the voices of all your former friends?

ELLEN. For spreading misinformation.

ISABEL. For daring to criticise you.

ELLEN. For systematically undermining the war effort.

ISABEL. What about freedom of speech?

ELLEN. What about protection of morale?

Another wave of pain.

Anyway, I was never a Communist.

ISABEL. No, you were a tourist, a Red weekender.

ELLEN. And you were never my friend.

ISABEL. Yes, I was.

ELLEN. You used me.

ISABEL. So?

ELLEN. So?

ISABEL. I can love you *and* use you. One doesn't cancel out the other.

ELLEN. Are you crazy?

ISABEL. Stalin needs me and any moment could – (*Puts two fingers to her head and makes a gun noise.*) We are vital *and* disposable. Both are true.

ELLEN. Well, that's mad.

ISABEL. No. That's fighting for something bigger than individual lives.

ELLEN. No. That's fighting for a megalomaniac who shoots his own followers in the head.

ISABEL. There's no getting through to you any more, is there?

ELLEN. Me? You've lost it, pal.

ISABEL. No, you have.

ELLEN. No, you have.

Beat. In spite of themselves, they smile.

ISABEL. I used to love the beginning of a cause. Licking envelopes, rattling buckets. They say hope is about 'the future' but hope is present tense, hope is people, being part of… That's what drew me to politics. But then there's nothing like politics to make you fucking hate people. It's like love, I guess. One minute it's simple as breathing. The next, you're a million miles away from each other and you don't understand a single word the other person is saying and no amount of talking will ever bring it back. And it makes you doubt whether it was even real in the first place.

ELLEN. I'm still fighting for equality, Isabel.

ISABEL. In Westminster?

ELLEN. It's the best we've got.

ISABEL. Ah.

Another huge wave of pain.

ISABEL holds a glass of water to ELLEN's mouth.
ELLEN drinks. It's a gentle moment.

ELLEN. Do you remember, in the Café Royal, when I was angry…

ISABEL. You'll have to be more specific.

ELLEN. The National Executive said we needed a 'clear narrative' for the Left?

ISABEL. Uh huh.

ELLEN. What if there isn't one?

ISABEL. What?

ELLEN is getting out of bed and putting her fire-watching uniform back on.

ELLEN. Me ne frego. That's Mussolini's mantra. I Don't Care. Now *that* is a clear narrative.

ISABEL. Shouldn't you wait for the doctor…?

ELLEN. But if your motto is 'I CARE,' tattooed across your forehead, frego, frego, well then, you'll constantly be a hypocrite, won't you? Because even the kindest most loving political act will always cause injury to someone, contradict something, forget something. The Left will always fail more frequently because…

ISABEL. Ellen, you're bleeding…

ELLEN. …it's a bigger job, and caring is complicated, so many things to care about, and the second we try to 'get clear', we reduce our ambition. It's not just a long game, it's the longest game imaginable…

Beat.

You see what I'm saying?

ISABEL. No.

ELLEN. It made sense in my head.

ISABEL. I am perfectly clear.

ELLEN. And *that* is why I'm scared of you.

ELLEN *is going.*

Take care, mate.

ISABEL. Ellen?

Beat.

To play a long game you need a long life.

ELLEN *touches the bandage on her head, looks at the blood. She puts her helmet on over her bandages.*

Exit ELLEN.

Scene Five

ELLEN *goes fire-watching with blood still streaming from her head. She runs around a bomb site, extinguishing small fires with her stirrup pump.*

She doesn't choose between fires; she puts out every fire. Finally, they are all out.

The scene changes around her. Several years pass. She takes off her bandages and wipes off the blood. She changes into her victory outfit. The war is won.

Banners appear above her: 'Victory', 'Cheer Churchill, Vote Labour' and 'Let Us Face the Future'.

Bunting.

Fireworks.

Music.

A chance for a new world.

Scene Six

Summer 1945. The night of Labour's victory celebrations.

HERBERT*'s house.*

ELLEN, *drunk, partied-out, triumphant, dishevelled, proud.*
HERBERT, *sober.*

ELLEN. Have a drinky drink, have a drink...

HERBERT. Stop shoving glasses in my hand.

ELLEN. Why aren't you ecstatic?

HERBERT. I'm not a schoolgirl. We have work to do.

ELLEN. Brilliant work. The work we've always wanted /

HERBERT. Attlee is going to handcuff me every step of the way, buffer me, box me in...

ELLEN *mops his brow with a tea towel.*

Get off.

ELLEN. Your sweat looks pink.

HERBERT. I need quiet.

ELLEN. Poor diddums.

HERBERT. Do you know how hard I have slogged?

ELLEN. Yes, darling, I did half of it.

Beat.

Men are astonishing. Truly. I'm trying to imagine a world in which I would literally sweat rage at the injustice of being a mere *deputy* prime minister.

HERBERT. You don't understand –

ELLEN. Oh really?

HERBERT. You don't know what it's like to have worked your whole life being consistently and ruthlessly prevented from achieving your full potential.

Beat.

What?

ELLEN. Never mind. I'm not exactly delighted with my
position either.

HERBERT. Why, what did you want?

ELLEN. Chancellor. Home secretary. Foreign secretary.
Something that fits with my life's work.

HERBERT. But you're the head head teacher. The chief of
chalkboards.

ELLEN. I beg your pardon?

HERBERT. You must be one of the top ladies in Britain now.

ELLEN. The chief of chalkboards?

HERBERT. It was a joke.

ELLEN. I'm the fucking Minister for Education.

HERBERT. Must you? I'm saying, you've been justly
rewarded /

ELLEN. *Rewarded?*

HERBERT. Are you planning to parrot everything I say?

ELLEN. It's your turn to make the tea.

HERBERT. Very well.

He makes tea like a martyr.

Milk?

ELLEN. Yes, obviously.

Beat.

HERBERT. Margaret's moving back from Cornwall.

ELLEN. Fine.

HERBERT. Just so you know.

ELLEN. I've always known.

HERBERT. So, she's moving back in.

ELLEN. She was evacuated, she never moved out.

HERBERT. Right.

ELLEN. Had to happen eventually. But we've talked about this.

HERBERT. Yes.

ELLEN. I've got my new flat in Dolphin Square. And we'll meet three or two times a week, discreetly, stay at mine. (*Shrugs*.) Easy.

HERBERT. You're so casual.

ELLEN. It's not romantic with her, is it? You are driving me a *bit* mad.

HERBERT. I forget you've done this before.

ELLEN. Hey there, buster, I'm the one accommodating *your* needs.

HERBERT. By demanding I lead a double life?

ELLEN. 'Demanding'?

HERBERT. I've been thinking.

ELLEN (*joking*). Risky.

HERBERT (*serious*). It is. Very.

ELLEN. If you can run the Home Office during wartime you can probably manage an affair.

HERBERT. I hate that word.

ELLEN. We've been having an affair for four years.

HERBERT. That was different. I didn't need to lie or creep about; 'sleep over' in some poky flat.

ELLEN. Poky?

HERBERT. I have decided /

ELLEN. You've decided?

HERBERT. I wish to begin this brave new chapter with a clean conscience.

ELLEN. So, you'll tell Margaret everything?

HERBERT. About what?

ELLEN. Us.

HERBERT. God, no, she'd be devastated.

ELLEN. Let me get this straight. Your wife is going to trundle back, with her suitcase and her hat-box, oblivious, and you'll greet her with a big kiss and snuggle up on that sofa, with a *clean conscience*?

HERBERT. As deputy prime minister, I need to set a moral example.

ELLEN. Everybody knows we're a couple...

HERBERT. The discreet understanding of our inner circle is quite different from the harsh judgement of the entire British public.

ELLEN. I wasn't planning a press conference, were you?

HERBERT. The tabloids turned a blind eye before, in the interests of morale, but now – especially given my new status – they'll be fishing for scandals.

ELLEN. Once a week, then. Occasionally.

HERBERT. I...

ELLEN. A kiss in the stationery cupboard.

HERBERT. We don't have a stationery cupboard.

ELLEN. Wait, so you want to end it *completely*?

HERBERT. Britain is expecting me to focus.

ELLEN. You're leaving *me*?

HERBERT. Stepping aside.

ELLEN *has a wave of pain.*

One of your headaches?

ELLEN. I worked tirelessly on your leadership campaign. Assisted every speech. Every thought. You couldn't have done any of this without me.

HERBERT. You were a great help.

ELLEN. Oh.

HERBERT. Don't be angry.

ELLEN. Oh.

HERBERT. You want me to be a respected leader, don't you? I'm doing this for us.

ELLEN. You're leaving me for us?

HERBERT. Do you want everyone whispering about you, sniggering into their sleeves whilst you try to lay down policy?

ELLEN. Don't you turn this on me.

HERBERT. You'd be 'the husband snatcher', the other woman, the home-wrecker. Do you think the Board of Education would listen to you then? Think of your health... your reputation...

ELLEN. Oh my God.

HERBERT. What?

ELLEN. This *is* about me.

HERBERT. It's not.

ELLEN. This is because of the smear campaign.

HERBERT. Not at all.

ELLEN. You can't associate with me now, is that it? And the horde of illegitimate children I popped out over the years in between my copious venereal diseases?

HERBERT. You know better than to pay attention to mud-flinging. They threw everything at us including the kitchen sink and they still lost by a landslide.

ELLEN. There's a special kind of mud reserved for middle-aged women and it sticks, Herbert – as you well know. No one cares about cheating men. We know at least ten blokes in senior positions whose mistresses bring them lunchboxes.

HERBERT. You don't bring me lunchboxes.

ELLEN. You don't bring *me* bloody lunchboxes. That's it though, isn't it? You're worried that *I* am going to sully *your* image?

HERBERT. That's... No, that's not it.

ELLEN. Then what?

HERBERT. You are extraordinary.

ELLEN. And?

HERBERT. But it's peacetime now... and... and /

ELLEN. I'm not the peaceful type?

HERBERT. Well...

ELLEN. Now that the bubble of war has burst. It was all so blissfully apocalyptic then, wasn't it? Kissing during a romantic blackout. Shells dropping rhythmically in the distance. But now the smoke has cleared, you run back to your stupid hand-woven wife.

HERBERT. Margaret is not stupid.

ELLEN. No, I am.

HERBERT (*ducking to avoid a flying plate*). Those are expensive /

ELLEN. Everyone loves me in a crisis. I'm an interlude. An adventure. But they don't want me in peacetime. In reality. Oh no. No one wants a crisis in an apron.

HERBERT. STOP THAT.

ELLEN. I'm the crisis woman. This is what I do.

HERBERT. Put the ashtray down.

ELLEN. I just want... a CALM NORMAL LIFE.

HERBERT. No, you don't. What am I, the third? The fourth married man you've been with?

ELLEN. And I never cheated on any of them.

She empties the bin over his head.

DON'T YOU LAUGH AT ME. All of you are married. You're ALL married. What am I supposed to do? TELL ME. Who am I meant to love? What about me? What about me? What about me?

HERBERT (*gently*). But you *don't* love me.

ELLEN. Then why am I crying?

HERBERT. Because you don't know how to give up.

Beat.

ELLEN. Where's my wife?

HERBERT. What?

ELLEN. Where's my wife that I can ship home to make me dinner and bolster my good name. Where's my fucking wife?

HERBERT. You're not making any sense now.

ELLEN. Just because you don't understand doesn't mean I'm not making sense.

HERBERT. Alright.

Beat.

Looks like a bomb hit it.

HERBERT *starts tidying.*

Perhaps you should move back in with Annie. I'm not sure you're strong enough to live alone.

ELLEN. You are not my father.

HERBERT. We have to work together, Ellen. Please. Dial back the emotion and /

ELLEN. There goes little Ellen and Annie. The invalid spinster sisters.

HERBERT. We've got a long road ahead of us.

ELLEN. You think I don't know that?

HERBERT. We must be mature: stop, breathe, think…

ELLEN. All I've ever had is *long road* /

HERBERT. …rediscover a certain restfulness.

ELLEN. You can't rest when you're born behind.

HERBERT. I don't even know what that means.

ELLEN. How could you? You're just another unremarkable, immensely powerful / man.

HERBERT. Change the record.

ELLEN. You CHANGE THE RECORD. It's your record. Over and over /

HERBERT. Please, I have neighbours.

ELLEN. HELLO DORIS.

HERBERT. You know what you need?

ELLEN. A chainsaw?

HERBERT. Thicker skin. You're taking *everything* personally and if I'm brutally honest, such hypersensitivity is simply not becoming of a government minister.

ELLEN. Wow.

HERBERT. You could get away with it as a kooky backbencher, but now – enough. I refuse to baby you through... whatever *this is* (which I know, sure as hell, is not really about me).

ELLEN. No, it's about *all* of you.

HERBERT. What does *that* mean?

> ELLEN *stubs out her cigarette on the carpet.*

> I think you should leave.

ELLEN. Men don't have thick skins – that's a myth – you have *role models*, everywhere, even on your worst day you can look to colleagues beside you, before you, and think: he survived so can I. History recharges you. Whereas I'm building on sand. I wake in the night with jeering in my ears... Men think they have self-belief but they don't, they have *proof*, allies, wives, children, stable homes, a whole structure built to support them – (*Coughs uncontrollably for ten seconds.*) even my own body is heckling me.

HERBERT. Ellen, you are the most powerful woman in the country. What more do you want? Fascism is defeated. For the love of God, stop the drama and do your job, your one job.

ELLEN. My one job?

HERBERT. The war is over.

ELLEN. Mine isn't.

Beat.

Mine isn't.

HERBERT. What?

ELLEN. Shhhh.

Beat.

Oh God.

HERBERT. Shall I get your nebuliser?

ELLEN. I don't care what you do.

For the first time in the whole play, ELLEN *goes completely still.*

I will never be chancellor. I will never be foreign secretary. I will never be prime minister.

HERBERT. One day, you might.

ELLEN. 'One day.' If you work really, really, really, really, miraculously hard.

HERBERT. Stick at it…

ELLEN (*to herself*). You can't even keep the job you've got. You're too tired. Oh Nellie, Nellie, Nellie. You've used your entire petrol ration just to get here. And he's still got a full tank.

HERBERT. You're talking to yourself.

ELLEN. And the long road is even longer than you thought. But you don't have any fuel left, do you?

HERBERT. Stop speaking in riddles.

ELLEN *goes.*

Oh, I'll tidy up, shall I?

ELLEN. It's your house.

ACT FIVE

Scene One

The LABOUR MINISTERS *are posing together for an official photograph.*

Nineteen men and one woman.

It's their house.

ELLEN *is sitting on the front row, far left.*

HERBERT *is also on the front row, fifth from the left.*

Ill and humourless, ELLEN *looks down the line at all of them – chummy, chatting and laughing.*

ELLEN *has never looked so small, and alone.*

PHOTOGRAPHER. Smile.

Scene Two

The Café Royal. 1946.

ELLEN. Napkins, shiny surfaces, no lipstick on my glass? This place has gone downhill.

OTTO. It used to smell of sweat and cheap wine.

ELLEN. Exactly, once it smelt of passion. Why are we here?

OTTO. You look lovely.

ELLEN. No, I don't.

OTTO. Your lovely, lovely face.

ELLEN. It's a long way to come from Mexico.

OTTO. I'm just passing through. I missed the drizzle.

ELLEN. Then what? You'll find another bunker?

OTTO. Something like that. How are you?

ELLEN. Don't bother. Mocking me.

OTTO. I would / never.

ELLEN. I am now a sworn-in member of the Privy Council.
I curtseyed to the king. Made myself even smaller, if you can
imagine that. Bottoms up.

OTTO. But your party is in power. Aren't you... happy?

ELLEN. They'll come to their Conversative senses soon
enough. And you say '*my* party' – but I don't trust any of
them, someone, or someones, left four copies of this
newspaper on my desk.

ELLEN *takes a newspaper from her bag and slams it down
on the table*.

'Ellen Must Go.' There's talk of a reshuffle, with my head
first on the block. Fair enough, though, really – I did wear an
'incongruous hat' the other day – to peals of merriment in the
House. And I lost the key to my own ministerial box three
times. Three. *That's* an achievement. 'Viva la revolution.'

OTTO. Your life is a revolution.

ELLEN. You're not recruiting now, pal.

OTTO. Do you remember our car chase? I thought my feet were
going to go right through that floor.

ELLEN. Oi, my motor was small but robust.

OTTO. What was it you used to say? 'I drive an Austin 7
because any bigger car would give the impression that it was
driverless.'

ELLEN. It's true. I rented a Cadillac once and you couldn't see
my head over the steering wheel. Pedestrians probably
thought a ghost was waiting at the lights. You know, I never
told you. We actually lost them on the ring road the first time
round but the second circling was purely for my personal
enjoyment.

OTTO. Red Ellen. The Mighty Atom.

Beat.

ELLEN. So, where *are* you going?

OTTO. Do you like my bow tie?

ELLEN. I do.

OTTO. You look very ill.

ELLEN. You look hollowed out from the inside.

OTTO. Two ailing spies.

ELLEN. I am not a spy.

OTTO. A working-class woman inside the walls of
    Westminster? If that is not espionage, I don't know what is.

Beat.

I have missed you.

ELLEN. Otto, is something wrong?

OTTO. Have you seen the movie, *Watch on the Rhine*? Lillian
    Hellman based the hero on me.

ELLEN. Seriously, where are you going to hide?

OTTO. From who?

ELLEN. 'From who.' The Guatemalan Highlands? Or back to
    Mexico?

OTTO. Oh yes. Trotsky was *so* safe in Me-hi-co. One morning,
    I might be feeding my rabbits in my 'sanctuary in exile'
    when some man arrives with a raincoat folded over his left
    arm and buries a pickaxe in my skull. No thank you.

ELLEN. Then what?

OTTO. 'Say your goodbyes' is a lovely English phrase, is it
    not? Goodbyes. Plural. Never just one. You must come to
    Prague one day. We will write a book. Of our heroic failures.
    Love in a Time of War. No, that's terrible. We can come up
    with a racier title than that. I'll put on my thought hat...
    thinking cap. My thinking cap.

ELLEN. You can't go home to Prague.

OTTO. I love Prague. The city of a hundred spires.

ELLEN. Stalin will kill you. You know too much.

OTTO. That reminds me of a joke. General says to Private: 'Have you come here to die?' Private says: 'No, sir, I came here yester-die.'

ELLEN. They'll torture you...

OTTO. It was so good to see you. I needed to see you.

ELLEN. There'll be a show trial /

OTTO. Let's not end on a dreary note.

ELLEN. They'll force you to confess to a thousand things you haven't done.

OTTO. What haven't I done? I love this word 'dreary'. Oooh, on the cover of our book, I'll be holding you in my arms like this.

ELLEN (*reeling from his breath*). Christ.

OTTO. I need to fix my teeth. They are the rubble of Europe.

ELLEN. You're giving up.

Beat.

Otto, I've spent my whole life running away from death. You can't just... saunter towards it.

OTTO. Forever a pleasure, Miss Wilkinson.

OTTO *does a little spin, and then bows.*

Do not let the bastards grind you down.

Exit OTTO.

ELLEN *looks at the newspaper. She rips it up into little pieces.*

Scene Three

The House of Commons. ELLEN has come back fighting.

ELLEN. The government has decided to make school milk free of charge in all primary and secondary schools. The government has also decided to make school dinners free of charge.

CHURCHILL (*from the other side of the house*). Can we be told the cost of these generous benefits?

ELLEN. I should be in a position to give an answer to the question the Right Honourable Gentleman is asking if it were put down on paper. Or it might be desired to wait until the Budget statement.

CHURCHILL. Is the Right Honourable Lady aware of the amount of milk that will be wasted?

ELLEN. There may be waste in isolated cases, but certainly not in general.

HERBERT. May I thank the right Honourable Lady for her statement which, I am sure, will be received with great joy everywhere?

ELLEN (*clear and true*). We do not deserve gratitude for deciding our children must not go hungry. Conversely, perhaps this House should apologise for taking so long. Some things, surely, are not complicated.

Scene Four

February 1947. It is the coldest and harshest winter in living memory, and there is a fuel shortage.

ELLEN*'s new flat in Dolphin Square.*

Enter ELLEN, *coughing, arms laden with pharmacy bags.*

Throughout the scene, she never takes off her coat, hat and gloves.

The phone rings.

ELLEN *answers.*

ANNIE *appears on the other side of the stage, speaking into the telephone, sitting beside the fireside in her Buckingham cottage.*

ANNIE. You're home.

ELLEN. Nice and early. And I went to the doctor's, like you asked.

ANNIE. Oh, thank you, thank you, thank you.

ELLEN. And I'm off the sherry.

ANNIE. You are?

ELLEN. Polishing my halo as we speak. You're right. I need to look after myself.

ANNIE. Gosh. I have waited my whole life to hear those / words

ELLEN. If my health suffers, my work suffers.

ANNIE *frowns.*

And work comes first. So, I'm wearing four jumpers, a thermal vest. And –

ELLEN *swigs from a bottle of cod liver oil. It's horrible.*

That was me swigging from a bottle of cod liver oil.

ANNIE. Are you meant to swig it?

ELLEN. Phenobarbital. Sodium Pentothal. Blah-de-blah-ital. I'm practically a walking medicine cabinet. Theamine for breathing, Amital for sleeping, penicillin for my little cough; the whole shaboodle. (*In a cartoonish voice*.) 'A United Front Against the Enemy Within.'

ANNIE. But you're taking it easy?

ELLEN. I'm fighting it off.

Another swig.

ANNIE. Hold on. *Four* jumpers?

ELLEN. It's freezing.

ANNIE. In your own flat?

ELLEN. Taking into consideration the current fuel crisis and the fact that in many factory offices clerical staff are working in overcoats /

ANNIE. You haven't lit your fire.

ELLEN. I'll use the kettle but that's it.

ANNIE. Ellen /

ELLEN. I gave my coal to the lady next door.

ANNIE. Of course you did.

ELLEN. What are you doing for Valentine's Day?

ANNIE. Feeding the cat.

ELLEN. Well, I was planning on sticking pins in my voodoo doll. But after that, shall we have a sisterly picnic? Indoors. With blankets and ginger ale?

ANNIE. It's a date.

Beat.

It's really nice to…

ELLEN. What?

ANNIE. I don't know. It's just nice.

ELLEN. Guess what?

ANNIE. What?

ELLEN. I've raised the school leaving age from fourteen to fifteen.

ANNIE. Wahey. That's extraordinary.

ELLEN. It's a start.

ANNIE. Put your fire on.

ELLEN. Night, night.

ANNIE. Sleep well, Nellie. Sweet dreams.

ELLEN puts the phone down.

ANNIE disappears from view.

ELLEN looks around at her nice new flat, entirely her own.

She puts the kettle on.

She takes out a huge pile of files.

ELLEN. Come on, Goliath, let's be having you.

She struggles to breathe.

She opens her prescriptions and swallows several pills from each (more than her prescribed amount but not dangerous).

She writes a Cabinet memorandum in response to a written question.

(*As she writes.*) The present scales of salaries for primary and secondary schools were submitted in accordance with Section 89 of the Education Act, 1944, to the Minister by the Burnham committee…

Time passes. ELLEN sings to herself, coughs, works.

She falls asleep at her desk.

An hour later. The kettle is burning on the stove.

She wakes up and runs over to the kettle.

Hell's bells. Agatha, your bottom is burning.

She laughs.

She gasps for breath again.

She takes another four pills.

It's not working.

She still can't breathe. She can't breathe at all.

I demand the... right to... breathe... Come on.

She punches her chest.

What can I do? Let's think about this. I need to... do
something.

*She takes a large handful of pills from each pill bottle. Far,
far too much.*

Not today!

She picks up another huge pile of files.

The files fall to the floor.

*She tries to pick up all the papers and reorganise them.
She can't. She picks up a random file and sits at her desk.
She can't keep her eyes open. She slaps herself in the face.*

Why isn't this working? This always works.

She slaps herself in the face again. It doesn't work.

Work.

She gets very scared.

Please work. Please...

Knock on the door.

She opens the door. There's no one there.

She closes the door.

Too dizzy to stand, ELLEN *tries to lie down on the bed. She
misses and pulls the bedcovers down onto the floor*

ELLEN *falls into a coma... we can only see her feet poking
out from behind the bed.* **The body stays there for the rest of
the scene.**

Another knock on the door.

ELLEN *enters from the other side of the stage.*

Enter DAVID.

David? Oh thank God. There you are. I came by, the week after the march, to give you back your key... but...

DAVID. I was dead.

ELLEN. But why, you idiot...

DAVID. Why?

ELLEN. You were so full of life! You had so much... left!

DAVID. I'm not sure you understand how death works, ma'am.

ELLEN. Oh, I understand alright. You were too young. And they'd worked you to the bone then sold you for scrap. How's that fair?

DAVID. Death isn't fair.

ELLEN. Too right, it's a ruddy disgrace. Someone needs to do something about it.

DAVID. Aren't you tired, ma'am?

ELLEN (*trying to return to her papers*). I just need to do a bit...

DAVID. You can't.

ELLEN....more.

DAVID. It's the end.

ELLEN. What are you talking about? It's taken us this long to get to the start. We'll march tomorrow, David, together.

DAVID. March where?

ELLEN. Do all the good we can... in all the ways we can. I mean, I know the weather's terrible /

DAVID. And you're dead /

ELLEN. But then the weather's *always* terrible. We'll set off first thing.

DAVID. It's time to go now.

ELLEN. Now? Even better. Great, yes, let's go now.

DAVID. Are you ready?

ELLEN. Not at all, look at me, I need waterproofs and... boots. (*Laughs*.) I need my tiny, tiny little boots...

The rest of the cast enter, dressed as MARCHERS. *They bring in waterproofs and boots for* DAVID *and* ELLEN.

Jarrow, Chester-le-Street, Ferryhill, Darlington, Northallerton, Ripon, Harrogate, Leeds, Wakefield, Barnsley...

ELLEN *dresses for the march.*

...Sheffield, Chesterfield, Mansfield, Nottingham, Loughborough, Leicester, Market Harborough, Northhampton, Bedford, Luton, St Albans, Edgware, Marble Arch, Hyde Park...

They gather around her.

...to the gates of power.

ELLEN*'s body is still behind the bed.*

ELLEN *and the* MARCHERS *hold the gaze of the audience for a moment.*

Blackout.

The End.

Afterword

After Ellen Wilkinson's death, all of her personal papers were burnt so no one will ever truly know what happened behind closed doors. This play is one interpretation. Although there are a few snippets of real speeches, 98% of her lines are fictionalised. It sounds like an Otto-ism to say 'the facts are not the truth' but a person's life is not a story – it contains multiple narratives colliding, intersecting, contradicting, and a cast bigger than any theatre in the world could budget for. My first draft was five hours long, packed with characters, linear, with not a single date altered, and as a result it didn't feel entirely true. However, after six years living with Ellen running around in my head like a ghost with unfinished business, I gradually found the confidence to tell this story.

There are a few deliberate historical inaccuracies made for the purposes of clarity and/or emotional narrative. For example, the KGB was not called the KGB in 1937 (and yet that is the acronym an audience will recognise) and Ellen's father actually died in 1929. All such decisions were made with much hand-wringing on my part but I took comfort in the knowledge that Ellen, more than anyone, knew the paradox of storytelling; that to dramatise a fact requires an element of cheek.

Another writer would have written a different play about Ellen Wilkinson – there are so many Ellens to choose from – but this is mine and it is a work of fiction based on fact, obsessive research, rumour, educated guesses, and individual experience. The poet Selima Hill once said, 'autobiography is not true enough. In order to be ruthlessly accurate, it is sometimes necessary to fictionalise' and perhaps the same principle applies to a biographical play. In order to get personal, I had to imagine the contents of Ellen's destroyed diaries.

Caroline Bird

Acknowledgements

Thanks to Lorne Campbell, without whom none of this would ever have happened. Wils Wilson for her dedication (and patience) and for transforming a script into a living, breathing creature. Kate Leys for her forensic dramaturgy; David Greig for his meticulous wisdom; Matt Perry for his invaluable academic input, and my agent, Emily Hickman, for supporting me through this epic journey. Thank you to the cast for activating all these words with their excellent minds. And of course, everyone at Northern Stage, The Lyceum and Nottingham Playhouse for maintaining their belief in this play in the midst of so many challenges.

Thanks to everyone who read and gave feedback on earlier drafts of the play: Andrew Cracknell, Hannah Silva and Paul Ratcliffe.

Thanks to my mum for reading every version and chatting with me into the small hours until a shape began emerging from the fog. Thank you to my dad for all the phone-calls and enthusiasm when I needed it the most.

Thanks to my beautiful wife-to-be Eliza. Your razor-sharp brain masterfully guided my thoughts when all I could hear was noise. I couldn't have done this without you.

Lastly and most importantly, thank you to Ellen Wilkinson. Working on this play has been one of the great privileges of my life.

C.B.

Bibliography of Research Material

Duchess of Atholl, *Searchlight on Spain*
Paula Bartley, *Ellen Wilkinson: From Red Suffragist to Government Minister*
Laura Beers, *Red Ellen, The Life of Ellen Wilkinson, Socialist, Feminist, Internationalist*
John Callaghan, *Rajani Palme Dutt: A Study in British Stalinism*
Peter Clarke, *The Cripps Version*
W.P Coates, *Anti-Soviet Lies Nailed*
Cato, *Guilty Men*
Claud Cockburn, *In Time of Trouble*
Claud Cockburn, *Reporter in Spain*
Edward Conze, *Spain Today*
Paul Corthorne, *In the Shadow of Dictators: The British Left in the 1930s*
Bernard Donoughue and G.W.Jones, *Herbert Morrison: Portrait of a Politician*
Kate Evans, *Red Rosa*
Sian Evans, *Queen Bees*
Adrian Fort, *Nancy, The Story of Lady Astor*
Pamela M. Graves, *Labour Women*
James Heartfield, *Unpatriotic History of the Second World War*
Lillian Hellman, *Watch on the Rhine*
Roger Hermiston, *All Behind You, Winston*
May Hill, *Red Roses for Isabel*
Ed. Mark Howe, *The Very Best of the Daily Worker*
Angela Jackson, *British Women and the Spanish Civil War*
The Labour Party Annual Report 1933
John Lewis, *The Left Book Club: A Historical Record*
Stuart Maconie, *Long Road from Jarrow*
Jonathan Miles, *The Nine Lives of Otto Katz*
Ivor Montagu, *The Traitor Class*
Tom Morton-Smith, *Oppenheimer*
James McGrath Morris, *The Ambulance Drivers*
Herbert Morrison, *The Communist Solar System*

George Orwell, *Homage to Catalonia*
Matt Perry, *Red Ellen Wilkinson*
Matt Perry, *The Jarrow Crusade: Protest and Legend*
Bernard Shaw, *The Apple Cart*
Bernard Shaw and Nancy Astor, *Selected Correspondence*
André Simone (Otto Katz's pseudonym,) *Nazi Conspiracy in Spain*
Graham Stewart, *Burying Caesar: Churchill, Chamberlain and the Battle for the Tory Party*
Betty D. Vernon, *Ellen Wilkinson*
The World Committee for the Victims of German Fascism, *The Brown Book of Hitler Terror*
Ellen Wilkinson and Edward Conze, *Why Fascism?*
Ellen Wilkinson and Edward Conze, *Why War?*
Ellen Wilkinson, *Clash*
Ellen Wilkinson, *The Division Bell Mystery*
Ellen Wilkinson, *Peeps at Politicians*
Ellen Wilkinson, *The Town That Was Murdered*

www.nickhernbooks.co.uk

 facebook.com/nickhernbooks

twitter.com/nickhernbooks